Tried and Tested Strategies: Removing Barriers to Learning in the Early Years

Angela Glenn, Jacquie Cousins and Alicia Helps

David Fulton Publishers

David Fulton Publishers Ltd
The Chiswick Centre, 414 Chiswick High Road, London W4 5TF

www.fultonpublishers.co.uk
www.onestopeducation.co.uk

First published in Great Britain in 2005 by David Fulton Publishers
Reprinted 2006

10 9 8 7 6 5 4 3 2

Note: The rights of Angela Glenn, Jacquie Cousins and Alicia Helps to be
identified as the authors of this work have been asserted by them in
accordance with the Copyright, Designs and Patents Act 1988.

David Fulton Publishers is a division of Granada Learning Limited, part of
ITV plc.

British Library Cataloguing in Publication Data
A catalogue record for this book is available from the British Library.

ISBN 1 84312 338 X

Typeset by Servis Filmsetting Ltd, Manchester
Printed and bound in Great Britain

CONTENTS

ACKNOWLEDGEMENTS

We would like to thank colleagues in Medway Pre-schools for their encouragement.

We would also like to thank Tony Faulkner, Manager of the Individual Children's Support Service in Medway Early Years and Childcare Department for his support. Thanks to the team, Fiona Macinnes, Tina Arterton, Sheila Hughes and Sue Oborne for their sound advice and for sharing expertise.

We would like to thank the staff at David Fulton for doing such a professional job with the series. We would like to thank Linda Evans for her continued friendly support and advice. Thanks to Jacey Abram for doing the illustrations.

INTRODUCTION

Children with special needs can teach us a lot about how to teach ALL children successfully and the skills gained along the way are invaluable for the practitioner. In the early years, the development of self-esteem and social skills is of paramount importance – especially for children experiencing any sort of difficulty within pre-school and nursery settings. Working on specific targets with a child in order to develop self-help skills and build up self-esteem makes a major contribution to overcoming barriers to learning – whatever they may be. It is important to remember that barriers to learning are usually constructed by the setting, rather than by the child himself. In this book, we have described some of the most common 'barriers to learning' experienced by children in the early years, and have made some suggestions about ways of getting over them.

The strategies outlined are a collection of ideas that may be adapted to suit a particular situation. Some of these ideas can be woven into the usual routine of the day, for example sharing learning objectives with children and using visual aids when giving instructions or explaining something.

Similarly, simple organisational techniques can really help very young children to understand the routine and make best use of the learning opportunities presented to them. Using approaches like the High/Scope 'Plan, Do, Review' system can also help young children make sense of what they are doing. Children are encouraged to think about and PLAN what they would like to DO and then to come together as a group to consider how the task actually went and what the outcome was as they REVIEW. This encourages a sense of responsibility and fosters feelings of self-control. It also gives the session some structure and predictability. This format is also an opportunity to model language and personal and social skills.

Identifying difficulties

When children encounter difficulties in an early years setting, it can be difficult to identify what the problem is and work out how to tackle it. It's important for practitioners to be aware of the huge range of achievements that make up the 'normal' scope of development. Developmental guides are useful (some are provided at the back of this book) but they should be used with caution – no two children are the same, they progress in different ways at different rates.

It isn't always easy for practitioners to identify accurately what the problem is and how to tackle it. Making a list of the things a child can do and the things he finds difficult can help. (See pp. 58–60 for guidance on observing children in the setting.) The Code of Practice for Special Educational Needs outlines four areas of difficulty:

- Communication and interaction
- Sensory and/or physical difficulties
- Cognition and learning
- Behavioural, emotional and social development

(Children with English as an additional language should not be registered on your Special Needs Register just because they are at the early stages of learning our language. These children should only be identified as having special needs if they have additional learning needs that can be categorised as significant. It is obviously a good idea for pre-school staff to be representative of the community in which they live so that communication with children and their parents is easier.)

Some children have a range of difficulties, crossing over these categories, and it can be hard to decide 'where to start' in supporting them. Involving advisory services, especially your Area Special Needs Co-ordinator, can help to identify problems and move the whole process forward. (See pp. 56–57 for more information about the Code of Practice and Individual Education Plans.)

Some children may have physical and/or medical problems which do not have a direct impact on their ability to learn. For these children, a Care Plan should be drawn up and agreed with the parent/carer and with all those working with the child.

All the ideas contained in this book are based upon tried and tested strategies that we have come across in early years settings over the years. Children with learning difficulties are likely to need a structured support system which is consistent and which THEY understand. The aim of this support is always for the child to develop his own learning style. Begin with the simplest and easiest things first, progressing to more intense/frequent/ expert help as necessary. Most of the ideas will not be new to you. Almost all of them are based on common sense and, when implemented into everyday practice, make for safe, enjoyable and successful early years settings that break down barriers to learning rather than erecting more!

(We have used the convention of referring to the child as 'him' and the practitioner as 'her' purely to avoid clumsiness in the text.)

SECTION 1

What are the barriers to learning?

Communication and interaction

Sensory and/or physical difficulties

Cognition and learning

Behavioural, emotional and social development

High/Scope approach

Games to improve attention and listening skills

All young children are born with a sense of curiosity about the world in which they live. Through learning, children develop essential survival skills and organise their world so as to make sense of it. They learn to acquire crucial 'building block' skills and also to regulate their environment which in turn helps them to live in a social world. For many, however, there are circumstances which can impede learning – especially if adults around the child fail to understand the difficulties he is experiencing and/or are unsure about how to take positive action.

Communication and interaction

'No man is an island' and children learn about themselves and the world through their interaction with others. Various theories have been put forward about this learning, including the importance of language, a staged 'readiness' approach and the importance of attachment between a parent and child. For children who have difficulties with understanding and using language, early years settings can be terrifying places! Imagine being left in unfamiliar surroundings with people speaking in a way you didn't understand. If you suspect that a child is experiencing this sort of difficulty, you need to consider the following course of action:

- Speak to parents/carers and find out what the child is like at home. What do they find works with him?
- Get advice from the Area SENCO and/or a speech and language therapist
- Speak slowly and clearly and support what you say with facial expression and gesture – a picture communication system may prove useful. (See PECS reference at the back of the book)
- Make eye contact with the child
- Be very specific when giving instructions; instead of saying 'Let's get ready for playtime', explain exactly what needs to be done: 'Let's put away the bricks now and put on our coats to go outside for playtime.'
- Make sure there is no hearing impairment – many children experience temporary loss of hearing through 'glue ear'
- If a child has autistic tendencies, there will be situations he finds difficult to deal with, for example lots of noise and running about; you need to be aware of this and find out how to manage it. A key worker will need to support the child and be sensitive to his needs

Sensory and/or physical difficulties

These sorts of difficulties are often the most straightforward to cater for and will usually have been identified by the health visitor/GP/parents. There may or may not be additional learning difficulties to take into account. Where the child has no additional problems, it is important not to allow the impairment in moving, hearing or seeing to limit the child's learning. This has a lot to do with expectations and encouraging the child to be as independent as possible. Wrapping him in cotton wool and doing everything for him will not be the best preparation for coping with the school environment later on. The other children also need to understand this.

In some instances, parents may not be aware of a sight or hearing impairment and it is only when in the early years setting that the child begins to experience difficulties. For example, parents may be used to speaking loudly and so the child with a **hearing impairment** does not struggle to hear them. At pre-school, with staff who have softer voices, and the added dimension of extra background noise, the child has much more difficulty. Look out for the child who:

- Does not follow instructions correctly
- Concentrates intently on the faces of people talking
- Copies other children
- Does not react to sudden noises
- Does not join in with rhymes and songs
- Talks too loudly
- Has delayed or indistinct speech
- Tilts his head when listening to a story
- Appears to be in a world of his own
- Has a discharge from his ear

A **visual impairment** may be noticed only when a child begins to learn to read and finds that the print is blurry. Look out for the child who:

- Holds books and objects close to his face
- Bangs into people and things, trips over objects
- Always sits at the front for stories or television
- Has difficulty with activities such as threading, which require good hand/eye co-ordination
- Has unusual eye movements
- Rubs his eyes a lot
- Holds his head in an unusual position

A child with **physical/motor difficulties** may:

- Seem to be very clumsy
- Have poor balance
- Have poor gross motor skills – find it hard to ride a trike, climb up the steps of a slide, kick a ball
- Have difficulty with fine motor skills such as threading, cutting out, drawing, fastening buttons

In these cases, parents should be encouraged to take the child to his GP who may arrange for a thorough examination by a specialist.

Once a child's difficulties have been identified, there is much that can be done to minimise the difficulties (see the 'Top tips' section on pp. 67–78) and a consideration of the setting's environment is a good starting point.

Looking at the physical environment:

- Find out if the child needs any special furniture or equipment – this can sometimes be borrowed from a resource base in the authority

- Have tables and chairs of different heights

- Make sure there is good light – natural and artificial

- Make sure there is enough space between tables and equipment for children to move around easily (and room for a wheelchair if necessary)

- Keep furniture and large equipment in the same place

- Do not polish floors

- Check that doors cannot trap children's fingers

- Keep cupboard doors and drawers closed

- Take care when opening windows that children cannot run into them

- Make sure toilets and washbasins are accessible

- Cover any sharp corners with foam

- Keep the floor clear of toys and small equipment

- Have handrails next to steps where possible (this may be a medium/long-term plan)

- Display pictures and labels at the children's height – clear, bold labels with pictures where possible

Cognition and learning

Most children will enjoy learning new skills and new ways of thinking and the learning process will be an enjoyable one for them. There will be some children with neuro-developmental or medical disorders for whom learning could prove more difficult and it will be important that the pre-school is able to support these children. There are support mechanisms and organisations within both Education and Health services, and where a child has significant difficulties, there is often a multi-agency team, providing support.

The biggest group of children identified as having special educational needs are those who, for a variety of reasons, learn at a slower rate than the average child. Two major issues with these children are likely to be lack of concentration and poor short-term memory. (At the end of this section are some activity ideas to help develop these areas.) There is often an overlap here, with difficulties like dyslexia or dyspraxia or autistic spectrum disorder playing a part. Look out for a child who:

- Scores poorly on baseline assessments compared with children of the same age
- Has difficulty in acquiring skills – particularly in communication and interaction, literacy and numeracy
- Has difficulty in coping with imaginative play
- Makes little or no progress in spite of positive intervention by staff in the setting

Developmental delay – slowness in reaching the traditional 'milestones' – may indicate learning difficulties, but may also be the result of poor stimulation and lack of learning opportunities. A rich early years experience can often 'kick start' developmental progress and enable a child to catch up with his peers.

Behavioural, emotional and social development

Perhaps the most powerful way of supporting any child in the early years is by focusing on emotional development so that the child feels confident about attempting new tasks irrespective of his situation or ability. This in turn leads to a high level of motivation and an increased capacity for learning.

Children with low self-esteem will see themselves as 'not very good' and may be reluctant to attempt tasks. This will be the child's way of preserving the little amount of self-esteem he already has, the reasoning being that you can't get it wrong if you don't attempt it.

All children have a basic need for wanting attention and wanting to please but this can be severely influenced by their emotional state or the way this is managed. Often, the child learns that one way of getting attention is by misbehaving, as for many children any attention is better than no attention.

This in turn leads to some form of punishment resulting in further low self-esteem and the cycle then repeats.

In many cases this cycle becomes a habit. The early years practitioner needs to recognise when this cycle exists and know how to change things.

In order to develop the child's self-esteem, it is useful to understand the kinds of behaviour we want to encourage.

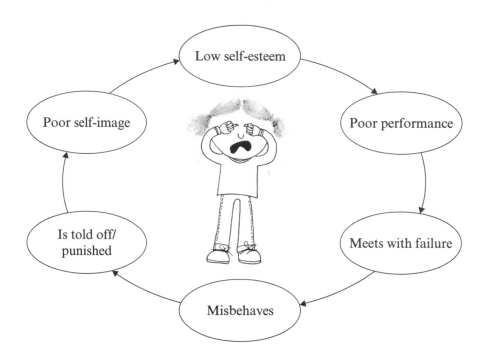

A child with high self-esteem will:

1. Volunteer information in a small group or whole group situation
2. Readily begin a task following individual instruction/group instruction
3. Participate in group activities, e.g. circle time
4. Complete tasks without undue reassurance
5. Play independently
6. Continue to respond in the face of change
7. Complete a task with one other person
8. Mix happily with others or will be happy to be alone on occasions
9. Respond positively to praise

Any of these points could be used as a focus – either as a general early years strategy to use with all children or as part of a specific programme for an individual child.

The next step might be to focus on a specific aspect of the child's development. In order to clarify his current level of self-esteem, the following checklist, aided by careful observation, may prove useful in determining which specific aspects of the child's emotional development need support.

Emotional development checklist

1. Does the child seem confident?

   ....

   ....

2. Does he enjoy new experiences and situations? Is he willing to 'have a go' at things?

   ....

   ....

3. What is his reaction to failure? Is he able to learn from mistakes, willing to try again?

   ....

   ....

4. Does the child constantly boast about himself and his own abilities? Does he make up stories to boost himself and impress peers?

   ....

   ....

5. Does he constantly ask for recognition and seek encouragement and positive feedback?

   ....

   ....

6. Is the child able to give his own opinions and express ideas? Does he wait until others speak and then agree with them?

   ....

   ....

7. Does the child belittle his appearance?

   ....

   ....

8. Is the child able to share or does he 'guard' personal possessions?

   ....

   ....

9. Is the child able to act independently and make decisions about things or does he need constant reassurance?

   ....

   ....

10. Is the child able to take responsibility for himself and his personal actions? Does he always blame someone else? Can he be given responsibilities?

    ....

    ....

The most effective way of developing self-esteem in a pre-school setting is by modelling behaviours likely to increase self-esteem.

Whole group strategies for enhancing self-esteem

How can adults help?

Children's self-image and self-esteem are enhanced by adults who:

- Act as models through their own positive comments about themselves (self-deprecating comments convey low self-esteem)

- Comment positively to and about other staff

- Show awareness of and interest in pupils as individuals

- Show genuine acceptance of children

- Devise rules and guidance with the children

- Allow some latitude and respect for individuals' actions within these limits

- Use the language of self-esteem when dealing with misbehaviour

- Project positive expectations of children

- Provide appropriate curriculum and feedback to child

- Provide honest appraisal (praise for effort is more helpful than praise for a picture which the child is not happy with)

Ways to help

- Catch the good in every child
  Let the child know every time you see him doing something good. Although this sounds tedious, the benefits are enormous and the child will be clear about expectations of behaviour.
- Praise effort as well as achievement
  Show the child you value his attempts – 'I know this is hard for you but you've made a very good start.'
- Make praise specific and genuine
  Tell the child exactly why you are pleased – 'I really liked the way you tried to put your own shoes on.'

- Praise every day

  This is very important for both you and your child. In this way you are looking out for good things he is doing and telling the child about it.

- Teach positive self-talk

  This can be a very powerful way of helping the child. You may need to start by pointing out all the good things you notice him doing. Gradually ask the child to start telling you things he has noticed himself. By encouraging the child to verbalise the good things he does you will be helping to develop a positive self-image and increase his self-esteem, e.g. 'I'm getting really good at doing up my zip.'

- Encourage positive statements about others

  Encourage the child to look out for and notice good things other people are doing and talk about them. Also encourage the child to comment on other people's good behaviours. This encourages an atmosphere of noticing and caring. Small group situations offer especially good opportunities for this.

- Provide constructive experience

  Use the child's own interests to develop learning. Find out from the child, parents or observation what the child's interests are.

- Use rewards

  This can vary from cuddles, smiles, and smiley faces to special individual time with an adult. Always try to tell the child when you notice him being good and explain exactly why you are pleased.

- Disapprove of the behaviour, not the child

  Always make sure that you separate the child from the behaviour so that the child recognises that it is the behaviour you disapprove of, not him as a person, e.g. 'When you kick Shaun it hurts him and makes him feel very unhappy. It also makes me feel very sad because I want to see the good boy that you are. I know that Shaun likes to play with you and you usually play very nicely together.'

- Use a when . . . then approach

  Another useful approach is to assume that the child will carry out the task you ask for. You can then provide a reward for the child complying with you. For example, 'When you've sat nicely and finished your sandwich then we'll choose a video and watch it together.'

Motivation

A child's motivation will be highly influenced by family and cultural values, and expectations. It is important to remember that you may have very little impact on what happens outside pre-school. What will be of absolute importance to the child will be the consistent, calm approach that you have at pre-school. For some children, this may be the most stable aspect of their lives.

Generally, motivation falls into two categories – *intrinsic* where the child does the activity for the fun and satisfaction of it, which brings its own reward. Most young children will enjoy most of the activities on offer and will learn through their play and creative activities.

For other children (or most children at some time) they will need a reward to carry out an activity. This is known as *extrinsic* motivation. For example, a reward may need to be offered for a child to sit with the group at story time until the child learns to join in independently. This could be a sticker placed under a cushion. If the child is able to sit on the cushion for an agreed length of time (possibly measured by a sand timer) then the child receives the reward of the sticker.

Attachment

All babies are initially totally dependent on their caregivers. As children develop they become aware that they are able to do some things on their own. They are helped to do these things by their caregiver and given encouragement when things go wrong such as when they fall over and can't get up again. This gives the child confidence to try again knowing that someone is there to help.

This period of development is usually marked by a strong emotional attachment that grows between caregivers and children, often referred to as a 'secure attachment'. This relationship will form the basis of all future relationships and learning. Securely attached children will play happily on their own, enjoy the company of both adults and children and accept change and new situations.

Clear signs that an attachment relationship has emerged with a specific caregiver are usually present by the end of the first year in normal infants.

A child with an 'insecure attachment' will find both learning and relationships difficult as they come into pre-school. Many of these children become too heavily reliant on adult presence and constant reassurance and may be unwilling to carry out new tasks or learn new skills. These children are likely to play with a very limited range of toys or activities.

It will be important for adults to be particularly aware of these children and to provide a highly nurturing environment where the child is able to feel secure and to develop his skills within the sensitive environment of the pre-school. Where possible, it would be helpful to model a nurturing relationship to parents by inviting them into the pre-school to see the positive involvement from pre-school staff. This could be done informally by inviting them into a 'play with your child' session or something similar.

For some children the pre-school may be their first experience of consistent management and a feeling of security. This situation may enable the child to feel comfortable and confident to try out new things and make mistakes that are regarded by staff as part of the child's learning.

High/Scope approach

A number of early years settings are now using the High/Scope approach to aid children in their learning. This approach is based on the idea that children learn best from active learning experiences, which they plan and carry out themselves.

High/Scope believes that children learn best in a play environment, which is stimulating but ordered. In early years settings the room is organised into interest areas, which are easily recognised by the children and are stocked with materials which are clearly labelled and sorted so that children know where everything is and can get out, and put away, materials for themselves. This also helps children to begin what they have planned to do independently, quickly and efficiently.

At home, children can also have a special place where their toys and books are kept and can be sorted into labelled containers to which they have easy access so that they can play independently.

A predictable routine helps children to feel secure and so they are able to learn with confidence. A routine also helps them to relate to time and sequence. Knowing what is happening next is important for children; it helps them to feel secure, helps them to learn about the passage of time and to remember things that are past.

In the early years setting each day the children:

- **PLAN** what they would like to do. Children begin by planning in a simple way; as they gain experience of planning they will talk about what they want to do, what they will use, where they will do the activity, possibly with whom they will do it and what they hope to achieve. An adult who will ask appropriate questions and give encouragement will support planning. Planning is a complex and valuable skill; when children become familiar with the techniques of planning they will use them throughout their lives, and at the early stage it encourages them to think before acting.
- **DO** whatever play activities they have planned using all the materials available to them. The role of the adult at this time is to observe the learning that happens naturally and to share in it, supporting children by playing alongside them.
- **TIDY** away the materials they have been using. It is an important learning experience for children; it develops their sense of ownership of, and responsibility for, looking after their environment. Tidying also develops mathematical understanding and an ability to co-operate with others.
- **REVIEW** their activities by telling (or showing in a variety of ways) other children and adults what they have done. In an early years setting this will usually happen with the adult and group of children with whom they did their planning. At home, children may talk about what they have done with family and friends.

Other parts of the High/Scope Daily Routine in early years settings include:

- Circle time. This is the time when all the adults and children sit together in a circle to share songs and rhymes.
- Small group time. In early years settings the High/Scope Daily Routine also includes activities which are initiated by adults. The children will work in

groups with carefully selected materials which will help them to develop learning 'Key Experiences'.

If you would like to know more about the High/Scope approach you can contact the High/Scope Institute in London at the following address:

High/Scope UK
190–192 Maple Road
London SE20 8HT
Tel: 020 8676 0220

Games to improve attention and listening skills

Kim's game

There are two ways that this can be played. Both versions require the following equipment: a tray; several different objects, small enough to fit on the tray; a cloth to cover the objects. Examples of objects could be a pencil, toy car, a key, teddy bear etc.

Version (A)

Place four or five objects on the tray (the number can be varied to make the task easier or harder). Show the child/children all the objects and talk about each item on the tray to make sure they are familiar with the vocabulary. Talk about the attributes of the objects and explain their use if necessary. NEXT, cover up all the objects with the cloth and ask the child/children to remember all the things that they saw on the tray. The time lapse between covering the objects up and asking the child to name them all can also be extended to increase the difficulty of the activity.

Version (B)

Again place about five of the objects on the tray and show them to the child. Ask him to close his eyes and then remove one of the objects from the tray. The child has to try to remember which one has been removed.

Grandma's shopping basket

This works on auditory memory and is best played in groups. One person starts the game by saying 'Grandma went shopping and bought some . . .' or 'John went shopping and in his shopping basket he put some . . .'. The next person has to remember the first item bought and add his or her own, e.g.

Child (1) 'Grandma went shopping and bought some bread'

Child (2) 'Grandma went shopping and bought some bread and some milk'

The game continues and the number of items to be remembered increases. The children also have to remember the order in which the items were bought. The game can be made easier by having a fixed number of shopping items (pictures or real things) placed on a table in the centre.

The children also have to remember the order in which the items were bought. This is a difficult game and can be made easier by having a fixed number of shopping items; pictures or real things may be placed on a table in the centre as visual reminders.

As an item is forgotten it can then be pointed out as a visual reminder. Signs and gestures can also be made up to remind the children of the objects, e.g. for milk, drinking could be mimed to prompt remembering.

Word stories

Pick two, three or four words for a child to remember (behind, in front). The child has to make up a story containing each word. The child then does another activity before trying to remember the story he made up and therefore the words he had to remember. Once the child can do this reliably, increase the length of time that lapses before he has to recall the words/stories.

Messages

A good way of working on auditory memory is by sending messages. Start by sending the child to another adult with a simple message to remember, and then increase the number of complexity of the things he has to remember. Word cards could be given to help cue memory.

Happy families

This is another game for a group of children. You can buy it in most toyshops. All the cards in the pack are dealt out and each child has to try to collect a family by asking other children (in turns) if they have certain family members.

Matching pairs

You can buy cards for this game from many retail outlets – or make your own pairs of pictures.

The pictures are shuffled and laid face down on a table. Each child has to take it in turns to turn over two cards to find a pair. If the two cards match they keep the pair. If they don't match, the cards are turned face down again. Children have to remember where different pictures were on the table in order to find more pairs. The winner is the one with the most pairs at the end.

Story building

This is another group game. One person starts off by saying one sentence of a story. The next person says the first sentence and then another sentence, increasing the amount of information to be remembered. Each child has to repeat the story so far and add to it.

Other ideas to improve memory of day-to-day events:

- Singing rhymes or chanting can be used to learn specific information such as days of the week, months of the year.

- Remembering day-to-day information can be helped by keeping a visual diary. Simple pictures showing activities done at school can be drawn in a diary at the end of the school day to prompt the child to remember. Parents can then ask the child about what he did at school. If he can't remember, the diary can be used as a memory aid. This idea can also be used to remind the child what will happen the following day to teach the concept of today, yesterday and tomorrow.

- Routines help the child to remember what to do:

    First we do   X

    Second we do Y

    Third we do   Z

- Colour coding things can help children remember where everything should be kept in the room.

SECTION 2

Case studies

1. A child who is highly dependent on adults for personal care
2. A child who cries persistently when leaving carer
3. A child who lacks confidence
4. A child with poor self-esteem
5. A child who finds building positive relationships difficult
6. A child who is unnaturally still and quiet
7. A child who is unaware of social norms
8. A child limiting his play experiences
9. A child who is unable to make connections or links between different parts of his experience
10. A child who is over-confident
11. A child who does not carry out instructions
12. A child with poor self-esteem who is unwilling to tackle new things
13. A child who dribbles or finds drinking out of a cup difficult
14. A child who uses a limited range of movements
15. A child who has difficulty carrying out activities requiring hand/eye co-ordination
16. A child who is not toilet trained
17. A child who is extremely active
18. A child who appears clumsy, bumps into things/falls over frequently and finds combining a range of movements difficult
19. A child who cannot negotiate stairs
20. A child who is intolerant to noise
21. A child who does not recognise colours
22. A child who is unable to differentiate between past and present
23. A child who lacks a sense of curiosity in the world around him
24. A child who plays with things inappropriately
25. A child who shows no interest in exploring objects
26. A child who avoids eye contact
27. A child who does not make her needs known
28. A child who has no language skills
29. A child who uses only single words
30. A child who lacks empathy for others
31. A child who fails to carry out instructions
32. A child with poor listening skills
33. A child who remembers little/nothing about stories etc.
34. A child who is hurtful to others
35. A child who is able to count by rote very well but appears to have no understanding
36. A child who doesn't recognise basic shapes and cannot match same shapes

CASE STUDY 1

A child who is highly dependent on adults for personal care

Sam has good motor skills and can play on the slide and bikes. He is able to use a paintbrush and enjoys the various activities at pre-school. His mother reports that he will not get dressed or do anything at home and just waits for people to get him dressed and to feed him. At pre-school he stands and waits for someone to take his coat off.

Possible reasons for this behaviour:

- Adults have resorted to doing things for Sam as it is quicker. He has not had sufficient opportunities to try things for himself
- Sam may feel that adults expect to do things for him and has developed a habit of waiting for people to do things for him
- Sam may feel that he is not very good in self-care areas and does not want people to see
- Could be the youngest in the family and may be teased for not being able to do these things

Strategies:

- At pre-school a focus should be on Sam taking his coat off on his own. Initially, he should be encouraged to do this with the adult so that he is fully aware of what to do. He should then be encouraged to do little things on his own, e.g. find the zip
- Reward Sam every time he attempts to do something on his own so he recognises that his skills of trying and independence are being valued. A 'Catch me Trying' chart may be helpful, where adults put a smiley face sticker on a chart whenever they see him attempting to do something
- Give Sam a special responsibility at pre-school so that he begins to see himself in a different light as being able to do things. In this way his self-esteem will develop
- Give him a 'peer buddy' who will help him and show him what to do
- Give him dressing-up opportunities
- Adults should avoid anticipating Sam's needs and should use every situation as an opportunity to develop independence

CASE STUDY 2

A child who cries persistently when leaving carer

George is described as being a very lively demanding boy at home. He is reported to be constantly 'on the go'. Whenever George is brought to pre-school he cries persistently and clings to his mother. He just stands by the door when his mother leaves.

Possible reasons for this behaviour:

- Attachment issues
- Wants/needs attention
- Finds the nursery situation frightening
- Has not been in a big group before and does not know what to expect
- George is anticipating that his mother wants him to respond in this way

Strategies:

- Encourage parent/carer to stay and sit alongside George. Gradually George's mother could leave for a few minutes and come back. Gradually she could go away for longer
- A toy from home might help George to settle
- Encourage a 'peer buddy' or friend who will look after George
- Use a visual timetable of the day where 'home time' is clearly highlighted so that George has a clear idea of what will happen and when

CASE STUDY 3

A child who lacks confidence

Megan found it very difficult to leave Mum when she first started at pre-school. She would cling and just sob. Megan's mother stayed with Megan for about three months. She now comes in on her own but immediately rushes to an adult and holds their hand. This has been happening for about three months. Megan will now engage with activities as long as the adult is there. Megan has two elder brothers who were confident, outgoing boys.

Possible reasons for this behaviour:

- She is the youngest child at home and has lots of adult attention and people doing things with and for her
- Megan enjoys adult attention and has learnt that this is a good way to get adult attention
- Megan is anxious when she is with children of her own age – possible difficulties in social and communication areas
- Megan has no previous experience of sharing and finds the whole situation noisy and frightening
- Attachment disorder to an adult

Strategies:

- Gradually encourage Megan to spend a few minutes of time on her own doing something she enjoys. Megan will need reassurance that the adult will soon return and should be rewarded with adult attention. It might be helpful to use a sand timer and start with one minute away. Megan could also be rewarded with a sticker. It may also be helpful to leave something belonging to the adult near to Megan, such as a pen or cardigan
- Try to engage Megan to play with or alongside another child with the adult present initially. Gradually the adult can be withdrawn for short periods
- Emphasise the 'big girl' aspect of Megan's development so that she recognises that she is being appreciated for being independent and 'grown up'. It may be that Megan feels she has to act in this way to gain adult attention. It may prove effective if she realises that adults are aware of her growing independence and will give her attention for that
- Encourage Megan to make choices about activities, e.g. 'Would you like to play with the Lego or do a drawing?' Giving Megan some control over what she does will encourage feelings of independence
- Megan could bring something of her mother's to pre-school and keep it with her during the session

CASE STUDY 4

A child with poor self-esteem

Zoe has just started at the nursery. She cries very easily and gives up very quickly when playing – other children just take toys away from her and she makes no resistance. She has started to just sit and watch others and shakes her head if an adult or child indicates that they want her to join in. She will not join in at snack time but has agreed to take her biscuit home. Zoe has two older brothers.

Possible reasons for this behaviour:

- Zoe may have got used to giving way to two elder brothers
- She has got used to being the only one at home in the day with her mother and likes playing on her own and dislikes and is puzzled by the routine in the nursery
- She may not be used to voicing her own opinions – she is never asked what she thinks
- Her opinion is not valued or given the same weight as those of other family members

Strategies:

- Highlight things Zoe is good at in the pre-school and share these with the group
- Ask an adult to work alongside Zoe while she is engaged in an activity requiring playing out definite roles. For example, playing shops – other children could be included, taking care not to allow children who are too dominant to boss her about
- If Zoe is alone and observing others – sit with her and help her vocalise what is going on, e.g. 'Tom should have said "please" when he took that toy from Joe, shouldn't he?'
- Use social stories about how to stand up for yourself
- Ask Mum if Zoe is quiescent at home and in other settings and see if she can encourage her to stand up for herself
- Zoe might need more time to settle but monitor regularly

CASE STUDY 5

A child who finds building positive relationships difficult

Tina often arrives looking anxious and glares at children or adults who approach her. Sometimes by the end of the session she is to be seen playing happily alongside others but the next day it is back to square one. She is invited to birthday parties but never wants to go and has been known to hide a party invitation from her mother.

Possible reasons for this behaviour:

- Tina is naturally wary of other children having been hurt by another child at a different pre-school
- She has little opportunity to socialise outside her current setting
- Tina is a member of a very small family who do not have large social gatherings or many visitors to their home
- Tina may find it hard to understand the rules of social interaction
- There may be a history of family problems, abuse or trauma
- Tina may have moved around a lot and has not had the opportunity to develop meaningful relationships
- She may be frightened to develop friendships because she has had previous relationships terminated in the past

Strategies:

- Give Tina plenty of time to watch and discuss what is going on around her
- Offer but do not insist on giving her a friend to play with
- Suggest to her mother that they go to the park nearby on the way home with a couple of other families and play on the swings
- Keep a careful note of the children she does eventually play with and make opportunities for them to do activities together without making it obvious
- Gently investigate with her mother the problems at the previous pre-school and if it is appropriate, do some circle time discussion or tell a story to raise the need for playing kindly etc.
- If autistic spectrum disorder is suspected then direct teaching of social behaviours may help
- When a new child joins the pre-school, ask Tina to help look after him and show him where things are kept

CASE STUDY 6

A child who is unnaturally still and quiet

Mollie is exceptionally quiet and has never been known to join in any lively activities. She likes to spend most of her time at the nursery in the home corner. She is small for her age and pale. Her elder brother who has now started school was also quiet but livelier than Mollie and had plenty of friends. Mollie is not unpopular but other children rarely notice her and do not expect her to join in pretend play. Her mother does not appear to be particularly concerned that Mollie is so quiet.

Possible reasons for this behaviour:

- Medical – Mollie may need referral to a paediatrician for a general health check
- There could be a hearing loss
- Mollie may have language processing difficulties
- Mollie could be suffering from anxiety – she could feel safest when playing with familiar toys
- She could just be a naturally quiet child

Strategies:

- Give her plenty of support and opportunity to do activities with an adult alongside
- Suggest to her mother that she gets her GP to refer to a paediatrician to check height, weight, hearing etc.
- Refer to speech and language therapist
- Try the 'peer buddy' approach
- Use puppets as a way of encouraging Mollie to join in with different activities – the puppets could be 'role models' for trying out new things
- Monitor closely

CASE STUDY 7

A child who is unaware of social norms

Billy has been at the pre-school for nearly six months and continues to shout, snatch things off other children and refuse to comply with simple requests such as putting his coat on to play outside. He seems to have only two volumes – loud and even louder. He is usually driven to the pre-school by his grandmother, often arriving late. They do not live nearby.

Possible reasons for this behaviour:

- Apart from the pre-school Billy may have little opportunity to mix with others and learn the rules of sharing and co-operating
- Billy may have a hearing impairment
- It is possible that he does not play outside often and is not used to putting on extra or different items of clothing. He usually leaves straight from his house, into the car and then into the pre-school
- It may be quite normal for Billy's family to communicate using very loud voices

Strategies:

- Explain to Billy's grandmother that it is important for him to arrive when the other children arrive – it will help Billy to know what is going to happen in the pre-school and also to experience how the others behave upon entry
- It is important to arrive on time in order to develop good habits for school entry, so adults working with Billy could encourage this by arranging to meet Billy first thing in the morning
- Check that Billy does not have a hearing impairment
- Billy will need to acquire the skill of using an appropriate voice, e.g. perhaps a 'table voice' and a 'pairs voice' could be demonstrated at snack time and an 'outdoor' voice could be demonstrated during outside play. Billy will need to practise these and become accustomed to the difference
- Using puppets may be helpful to encourage more appropriate behaviours
- Social stories could be used to illustrate how to 'make friends' etc.

CASE STUDY 8

A child limiting his play experiences

Daljit is a well-dressed, chatty boy who regularly engages adults in polite conversation. However, he shows no inclination to play with anything else other than a set of stacking toys. Neither does he seem keen to join others in the sand and water or have a go on any of the larger wheeled toys in the garden.

Possible reasons for this behaviour:

- Daljit has not had the opportunity to play with 'messy' activities
- He may live in a flat with no outside play area
- He may have few playmates outside the pre-school
- He may come from a family who do not encourage physical risk-taking and are worried about him hurting himself
- Daljit may not like the feel of sand or playdough etc.
- His mother may not like him to get dirty

Strategies:

- An adult could play alongside him, gradually increasing the range of activities
- Move the stacking toys nearer or in the same box as other equipment and introduce other varied 'clean' activities
- Talk to Mum about range of activities at home
- Warn Mum when painting or other messy activities are on the agenda so that she can dress Daljit in some old clothes and assure her that aprons are available
- Suggest to mum that she collects him early on some days so that she can see the range of activities on offer
- Make sure that Daljit has plenty of opportunity to use a pedal car or climbing frame with adult help at first and then independently
- Make the outdoor area really exciting and use as many natural climbing and balancing objects as possible, e.g. large logs, rocks etc.
- Let Daljit share a catalogue with an adult and another child to talk about what they like doing

CASE STUDY 9

A child who is unable to make connections or links between different parts of his experience

Christopher has not really made meaningful relationships with the adults in the pre-school. Although he recognises and uses the correct name for his key worker, he does not relate to her in the same way the other children do. One day, the children were looking at some photographs of themselves as babies. Christopher appeared not to recognise himself and did not have any 'baby stories' to tell in spite of the fact that his mum had just had a baby. Christopher tends to avoid interaction with the other children, he never volunteers information in circle time and never mentions events that occur at the weekends or in the holidays.

Possible reasons for this behaviour:

- Christopher may have a limited vocabulary
- He may prefer to keep home and school separate
- Christopher has suffered some sort of trauma
- The family may have experience of input from agencies and the children have been told not to say much about home
- He may just be very shy with adults
- He has got a different regional accent and will speak when he feels confident
- He has a memory problem
- Possible learning difficulty and/or speech and language disorder

Strategies:

- Talk to Christopher about what will happen during the session and use visual aids/timetables
- Give him the opportunity to share news but do not force the issue
- Make sure there are opportunities to talk on a one-to-one basis and in small groups as opposed to the larger groups
- Use visual aids (real objects whenever possible) when you talk to Christopher, especially to help with self-help skills that will need sequencing, e.g. personal hygiene, washing hands etc., and share this with the home
- Talk about events that have just happened in the pre-school and encourage Christopher to talk about what he has done
- Keep a pictorial diary of Christopher's activities so that he can take it home to show Mum – he will need help with this at first but may carry on with this when he gets older to help structure his time
- Over-learning and repetition may be helpful

CASE STUDY 10

A child who is over-confident

Alfie always insists that he is able to do things even if it is a completely new task. He will rush at tasks, not waiting for instructions, and will often exclaim, 'I'm really clever, aren't I?' or 'I'm the winner.' He doesn't always respond appropriately to instructions, appearing to prefer his own agenda. At group times, Alfie always puts his hand up (sometimes before the adult has finished speaking) to indicate that he knows the answer (even when he doesn't). Alfie throws himself into physical activities with an over-enthusiasm bordering upon recklessness.

Possible reasons for this behaviour:

- Alfie truly lacks any idea of what constitutes a 'good' performance
- He does not notice what his peers are doing
- Alfie's parents may over-praise when he is at home
- Alfie may have an inappropriate amount of power in the home
- He may be the youngest of much older siblings or an only child who is being indulged
- Alfie may have attention deficit disorder (ADD) or attention deficit hyperactivity disorder (ADHD)

Strategies:

- Alfie will need to be praised only for things which are worthy of praise–the aim of this being that he will learn to recognise this for himself. Questioning along the lines of 'Is that sensible?' or 'What can happen when you do . . . ?' would help
- Alfie should be praised when he behaves appropriately but ignored otherwise
- He should have the opportunity to talk about what he is going to do and to think clearly about HOW he will do it
- Alfie will need to acquire the notion that the adults in the pre-school are in charge and even though he may not have to conform at home, he will have to stick to rules in the setting. It might be useful for him to think about what will happen if he sticks to rules and what will happen if he does not – and to make 'good choices'
- The High/Scope approach would be useful

CASE STUDY 11

A child who does not carry out instructions

Although pre-school staff feel that Connor enjoys activities when he does them, Connor's usual response is to say 'I'm not going to do that.' This happens with a range of activities and staff feel that Connor would really like to become involved but that he is stopping himself.

Possible reasons for this behaviour:

- Connor likes to control situations around him
- He has learnt that he receives more attention when he says he can't do something or if he refuses to do it
- He may not fully understand the instructions so it is 'safer' to refuse to do it
- He may be used to doing what he likes when he likes, so conforming to instructions may be new and unwelcome

Strategies:

- Allow Connor a choice in his activities, e.g. he can choose to do a painting or to play with Lego. In this way he will have a level of control over the activities he chooses
- Make sure that instructions are simple, i.e. contain one instruction at a time and give time for processing
- Let Connor consider a number of activities he would like to complete during the session. A review period should follow this
- Do not give Connor any attention until he has completed the activity. Use a statement such as 'When you finish your painting, then I will sit with you and we can read a story together.'
- Give attention for positive wanted behaviours and ignore Connor if he behaves inappropriately

CASE STUDY 12

A child with poor self-esteem who is unwilling to tackle new things

Jack holds onto his mum's hand for as long as he can when leaving her in the morning. He has some favourite, limited activities and usually chooses to play with these. Whenever the routine has been changed, he will sit quietly, on his own, watching the other children. Jack does not like to get dirty and prefers not to do hand printing or other things involving making a mess. When the pre-school got their new climbing frame and slide out, Jack said that he did not want to go on it but watched the other children playing. If adults ask Jack if he would like to try out a new activity he usually says 'No'.

Possible reasons for this behaviour:

- Jack is a very shy and quiet child
- He is insecure
- He lacks confidence
- He may think that he has to keep clean and tidy
- He may have had a bad experience while using large apparatus such as slides etc.
- He may come from an environment at home where there is anxiety about new experiences and physical challenges

Strategies:

- Find out what Jack's interests and strengths are and use these to build his sense of curiosity
- Give lots of encouragement about his achievements
- Team him up with children who will help him and present him with good role models
- Introduce him gently to new things, one at a time, and show him how much fun things like the climbing frame are
- Never try to force Jack to do things he finds unappealing

CASE STUDY 13

A child who dribbles or finds drinking out of a cup difficult

Kim enjoys all the play activities at nursery. All the children in her group now use a proper cup for drinking but Kim cannot seem to manage this. She still needs a lidded beaker. Nursery staff have noted that Kim's T-shirt is often wet with her dribbling during the session.

Possible reasons for this behaviour:

- Oral motor skill difficulties
- Little or no practice in using an open cup
- Is this reflective of other motor skill difficulties (dyspraxia)?

Strategies:

- Speak to parent/carer about Kim using a cup at home – encourage them to introduce a cup if this has not already been done
- Parents and nursery staff may need to seek advice from a medical practitioner and/or a speech and language therapist
- If medical reasons have been eliminated, nursery staff and parents could work on a programme together to develop oral motor skill. This might involve blowing bubbles into the air, blowing through straws to make bubbles in water, tongue exercises etc.

CASE STUDY 14

A child who uses a limited range of movements

Ahmed has an unusual gait and often appears uncomfortable when doing physical activities. He is reluctant to use the climbing apparatus and takes a lot of persuading to join in any ball games. He is very definitely left handed and is beginning to write his name. He loves listening to stories.

Possible reasons for this behaviour:

- Physical weakness on the right side
- Poor eyesight in one eye
- Inner ear problem affecting balance
- Lack of experience/encouragement to take part in physical activities

Strategies:

- Ask parent/carer to arrange for a medical assessment, eyesight and hearing tests via GP
- Plenty of opportunities to practise using both hands
- Provide a wide range of equipment, including large apparatus, so that opportunities are available to practise a variety of movements and skills indoors and out
- Careful observation and monitoring

CASE STUDY 15

A child who has difficulty carrying out activities requiring hand/eye co-ordination

Leanne really tries hard to join in with all the activities in the pre-school. She seems to enjoy using all the equipment but has difficulties with things like threading beads, using a peg board, cutting out and using a pencil. Although she enjoys the pre-school, she is starting to become frustrated with her lack of ability in the above activities. She is a bright child and is aware that her friends can do these things with much more ease. Leanne has started to avoid the activities she thinks she is not good at.

Possible reasons for this behaviour:

- There is a physical reason which may need investigating
- A visual problem
- Lack of experiences in this area

Strategies:

- Ensure that there is a wide range of equipment in the pre-school and at home to enable Leanne to experience manipulative skills, e.g. cooking, playing musical instruments
- Provide equipment in differing sizes, e.g. brushes, pencils, beads, weaving etc.
- Provide equipment specially designed for children with weak grips, for example early scissors and easy-to-use tongs for practising picking up items of varying sizes
- Keep providing opportunities for practising manipulative skills and that these are ongoing for children slow to develop them
- Provide opportunities to practise gross motor skills and let children take part in vigorous exercise before asking them to do something more formal
- For some skills like cutting, it may be a good idea to actually hold Leanne's hands in the right way and guide her at first so that she gets to know how it should feel
- Short but frequent practice sessions on a particular skill would help
- Don't forget to point out what Leanne is good at and praise her when she has made a good effort at the things she finds difficult. (It might be worth pointing out that everybody finds something difficult)

CASE STUDY 16

A child who is not toilet trained

Chloe likes the pre-school and joins in with all activities. In contrast to her peers, she still wears nappies and does not indicate her needs regarding toileting. Chloe will be starting school soon and the staff in the pre-school are concerned about her lack of interest in using the toilet. Her mother reports that Chloe refuses to use a potty or the toilet at home.

Possible reasons for this behaviour:

- A physical reason for the delay
- Chloe doesn't see the necessity to become toilet trained
- Chloe's mother doesn't view it as important (or does not know how to go about it)
- Not developmentally ready

Strategies:

If a referral to the GP found nothing significant then:
- Talk to Chloe's mother about toilet training and why it is important for Chloe to use the toilet independently in readiness for school. She may need some advice about training – suggest contacting the Health Visitor
- Devise a plan which can be carried out at home and at the pre-school, with regular times for sitting on the potty/toilet
- Make sure that Chloe is comfortable when sitting on the potty/toilet – with feet on the floor or a box. Stay with her
- Use lots of praise when Chloe 'performs' on the potty/toilet
- Show Chloe how the toilet works – some children are frightened of the flush
- Make sure that Chloe is wearing easy/to/undo and pull/up clothing
- Check other developmental areas, as toileting difficulties may be reflective of other areas of Chloe's functioning

CASE STUDY 17

A child who is extremely active

Daniel is always on the go. He is bright and quick on the uptake but is reluctant to conform to any instructions and cannot stay on task for more than a couple of minutes. He is very demanding of adult attention, calling out for people to look at him while he rides a bike, does a painting etc. Although other children often laugh at his antics, they are becoming increasingly reluctant to play with him as his staying power is so limited and it is impossible to play a game or share any equipment with him. His mother reports that he is just as demanding at home and she freely admits that the pre-school keeps her sane! She says he hardly needs any sleep and is always up at the crack of dawn.

Possible reasons for this behaviour:

- Possible attention deficit hyperactivity disorder (ADHD)
- Lack of firm boundaries and consequences at home
- Inappropriate diet – it is possible that E numbers do not help

Strategies:

- Firm and consistent rules and consequences
- Positive attention – notice when he is doing the right thing and tactically ignore the unwanted behaviour
- Discuss with his mother the need for a referral to a paediatrician in case ADHD is the cause of his high level of activity
- Carry out some detailed observations to aid any medical diagnosis
- If Daniel's behaviour is impacting upon his progress with learning then some small steps with measurable targets should be set for an IEP
- If his learning is not affected then a behaviour management plan should be considered

CASE STUDY 18

A child who appears clumsy, bumps into things/falls over frequently and finds combining a range of movements difficult

Harry is a big boy for his age. He has been at nursery for three terms and will be starting school next term. He is friendly and outgoing and other children like him. He has not yet managed to learn to ride a tricycle, although he has tried hard. He often trips up, drops things and knocks into equipment. He can recognise his own name but cannot yet manage to write it. He rarely chooses to do any pencil and paper activities. Games involving hopping and jumping in a sequence are hard for Harry and he often loses his balance. His mother reports that he cannot manage to get dressed by himself and she is worried about him starting school where he will be expected to get changed for PE activities.

Possible reasons for this behaviour:

- Developmental delay
- Poor eyesight
- A physical problem affecting the middle ear
- Dyspraxia
- Lack of opportunity to practise skills, e.g. mother getting him dressed rather than encouraging him to have a go for himself

Strategies:

- Allow Harry more time than is usual to try activities for himself
- Suggest to his mother that she gets him checked by the GP
- Give plenty of opportunity to practise gross motor and then fine motor skills
- Encourage Harry to practise a range of skills to improve hand/eye co-ordination, e.g. threading, puzzles, dot to dot etc.
- Get him to hop, skip, run etc. along pathways drawn on the floor and suggest to his mother that you all work on the same activity at home and at nursery
- Physical activities involving large movements with arms crossing the midline of the body in big circular movements help – *Brain Gym* is a book which goes into some detail and is full of activities for children with motor co-ordination difficulties
- Dance classes or 'circuit training' sessions can help
- Make sure there is plenty of access to an outdoor area where large brushes could be used to make giant shapes on walls or the ground with water. Also, large apparatus should be available to encourage physical development and exploration, with children being able to go out whenever they like

CASE STUDY 19

A child who cannot negotiate stairs

Gordon likes the large equipment like pedal cars and tricycles. He seems to have real difficulty whenever confronted with either one step or stairways. Even though he is obviously looking at the steps very closely, Gordon seems unbalanced. Gordon always needs to either hold onto an adult's hand or will bottom shuffle down the stairs. Going down is more difficult for Gordon, although climbing them is also a slow process because Gordon does this very deliberately, one step at a time.

Possible reasons for this behaviour:

- Gordon has depth perception problems – he cannot judge the height and depth of different surfaces
- There may be a sensory problem, e.g. visual problems
- There may be a lack of opportunity to practise this skill

Strategies:

- An assessment in sensory perception/vision would help to ascertain whether there is a problem. Are glasses needed?
- Can a hand rail be fitted to steps at the setting?
- Practise going up and down steps by using a small box or bench. Make the steps small at first. Practise going one step up and one down at first and then gradually increase the number of steps and the height and depth. Use adult support at first, then see if Gordon can practise independently

CASE STUDY 20

A child who is intolerant to noise

Nicholas comes into the pre-school before the other children because he does not like to come in with all the others and always clings to his mother. At pre-school he usually sits in the guest area and looks through the books. He sometimes watches some of the other children as they play chase and ride their cars around. As soon as it gets noisy, Nicholas covers his ears and closes his eyes and starts to nod his head up and down.

Possible reasons for this behaviour:

- Nicholas has a very quiet home environment and finds the noise and lively atmosphere frightening
- Nicholas has a particular sensitivity to sound which may require further medical investigation
- This is Nicholas' way of saying he does not like being too near other children
- Speech and language/autistic difficulties

Strategies:

- Investigate the possibility of a medical or physical reason
- Assess the quality of Nicholas' speech and language skills and if a problem is suspected, ask for a speech and language assessment
- Allow Nicholas time to just watch. He may need longer than other children to become familiar with pre-school activities
- Introduce a friend who will play with Nicholas for certain parts of the session. Initially, these could be the quiet times, gradually introducing a friend into group situations
- It may be helpful to find out how Nicholas interacts with others in the home setting and whether he understands how to play with the other children
- He may need direct teaching about how to join in games and how to use the equipment
- Situations may need to be specifically set up in order to encourage interaction – this could be very simple at first, e.g. rolling a ball to and fro with one other child and then gradually involving two and three other children. Staff should be aware of how comfortable this is for Nicholas and be guided by this as to how quickly (or slowly) they proceed

CASE STUDY 21

A child who does not recognise colours

Raj has been at the pre-school for nearly a year and cannot identify the three primary colours. When he paints a picture, he will use any colour indiscriminately. If the activity requires the correct use of colour, for example if the task involves close observation of things like plants etc., Raj will use inappropriate colours every time. When an adult asks Raj what colour trees are, he will seem puzzled and will answer 'I don't know.'

Possible reasons for this behaviour:

- Raj is colour blind
- Raj has not learnt what the names of colours are
- He has a problem with vision generally

Strategies:

- A check with the health visitor/GP could ascertain whether or not Raj is colour blind or has any visual impairment
- If the above are not an issue – Raj needs some intensive teaching on the names for colours
- Starting with one of the primary colours, Raj will need to be able to identify this in a range of contexts, e.g. Raj is wearing blue trainers, socks etc. He should be able to collect blue items and put them in a box, identify the colour blue in a range of settings and be able to transfer this knowledge to familiar and unfamiliar situations – this process needs to be over-learnt until secure and then repeated for other colours
- If Raj has particular difficulty with one colour – move on to another and come back to the first later

CASE STUDY 22

A child who is unable to differentiate between past and present

Noel is enthusiastic about all the activities in the pre-school. It has been noticed that Noel muddles up times and events and, at first, adults took this to be part of normal development. However, Noel still continues to do this even though his peers are starting to differentiate between what happened yesterday and what is happening today. Noel will say things like 'I am doing a painting yesterday.' When asked about significant events like his birthday, Noel will become muddled and appear not to understand that his birthday was last week, although he can remember having a party.

Possible reasons for this behaviour:

- Noel has a memory and/or sequencing problem
- Noel's vocabulary and understanding of concepts have not yet developed to include terms like 'yesterday', 'today' or 'tomorrow'
- Noel has had few opportunities to talk about and secure events that have happened

Strategies:

- Noel will need to be provided with opportunities to play memory games (like Kim's game) and games involving putting pictures into the right sequence. This could be very simple at first, with just two or three pictures. The number of the pictures and the difficulty could be gradually increased. You could use photos of Noel's life, e.g. pictures of him as a baby, toddler and so on for him to sequence
- Activities should be accompanied by the correct vocabulary, e.g. 'You did the painting of the car yesterday and you are playing in the sand today.'
- Use significant events like birthdays to reinforce the correct use of terms to indicate past and present
- Further vocabulary indicating past and present, like 'before' and 'after', should be introduced gradually when Noel has made some progress

CASE STUDY 23

A child who lacks a sense of curiosity in the world around him

Ross walks into pre-school happily and immediately walks over to the trains. He would play with the train set all day long and insists on taking a train with him wherever he goes. Pre-school often go on outings to the local shops and park but all Ross ever wants to do is sit alone with his train; he gets very upset and it is very difficult to calm him. In spite of efforts to engage Ross in other activities, he seems completely uninterested.

Possible reasons for this behaviour:

- Ross does not have a train set at home and wants this one all to himself
- Ross has obsessive characteristics which can be typical of children within the autistic spectrum
- There may be anxiety issues which affect Ross' behaviour

Strategies:

- Use the train set as a reward when Ross experiences a very short activity, e.g. Ross can keep the train in a backpack when he is on the swing and then can play with the train afterwards
- Ross may be a particularly anxious child who may need the security. When Ross is ready, perhaps he would hold a smaller train or a picture of a train. Maybe the train or picture could then be put in his pocket
- Check for other symptoms and if there are still concerns, ask for a medical opinion with parents' permission

CASE STUDY 24

A child who plays with things inappropriately

Alfie is a sociable boy whose attendance at the pre-school has not been very regular. The family frequently holiday with relatives around the country and he often turns up unexpectedly. He is popular with the other children, although he can play quite roughly (but not unkindly). An older sister, whom he is happy to see, usually collects him from the pre-school. He tends to drift from one activity to another and will wander off with equipment and will readily use a book as a shovel in the sand or use felt-tip pens in the water. He is often quite put out if an adult asks him not to wander about waving the scissors around and appears genuinely puzzled.

Possible reasons for this behaviour:

- Possible lack of experience and/or boundaries – may not have pens and paper at home or he may be allowed to use kitchen items in the garden. He may not be expected to sit at a table to eat so wandering off may be quite acceptable at home
- It may be that Alfie spends little time in one place and he may not have many of his 'own belongings' – it may be that family members improvise with household items and use them as toys whenever Alfie comes to stay

Strategies:

- Provide lots of good role models and ensure that all adults give specific instruction and demonstrate the use of scissors, safe use of equipment etc.
- Talk to parents/carers about the need to explain how to use equipment safely and appropriately
- Provide opportunities for pretend tea parties etc.
- Make sure equipment is stored appropriately, EVERYONE holds scissors correctly, items are kept in labelled trays etc.
- Use rule reminders (e.g. we play carefully) rather than just telling him off

CASE STUDY 25

A child who shows no interest in exploring objects

Harrison loves to look at lights and lampshades. He will spend a long time just looking at the lights in the pre-school. He also likes to look at his fingers and holds them up to the light and looks through them. He shows no interest in handling objects or playing with them. If an object or toy is placed in front of him, he will look at it but does not touch it unless he is familiar with it. He particularly likes battery toys that light up.

Possible reasons for this behaviour:

- Does not like the feel of many items
- Has physical difficulties handling objects
- Has significant learning difficulties
- Has a sensory disorder

Strategies:

- A sensory/paediatric assessment would be helpful. (Ask parents to arrange with the GP)
- Use Harrison's interest in lights as a starting point. He may benefit from a sensory room type environment where he follows a light to lead to an object of interest, e.g. food
- Harrison may need to be taught the skills to create cause and effect in an activity or toy
- Harrison may need to feel more relaxed when handling items. Soft background music may prove beneficial
- Ask parent/carer about Harrison's behaviour at home – he could bring toys from home if it was felt to be useful

CASE STUDY 26

A child who avoids eye contact

Kelly does not look directly at anyone while they talk to her. When her key worker is giving instructions, Kelly will just carry on with an activity or appear to look into the 'middle distance'. Most of the time, she does carry out instructions if they are not too complicated. Very occasionally, Kelly will make fleeting eye contact whilst making her needs known to an adult. Kelly usually plays with one other child, Milly, with whom she has formed a strong bond, and will become upset if she is not at school.

Possible reasons for this behaviour:

- Kelly is just a very shy child and finds looking directly into people's eyes threatening
- There may be a cultural difference where looking directly at adults is not acceptable
- Possible autistic spectrum disorder

Strategies:

- If there is no cultural reason for the behaviour – encourage Kelly to look at the speaker's fringe or glasses in the first instance
- Use gentle reminders about looking towards the person's face and do not start to speak until Kelly has turned towards you
- Every time Kelly uses eye contact – acknowledge this in a low-key manner
- Wear a fun hair grip or even something more outrageous if appropriate to encourage Kelly to look at you (Christmas is a good time to do this – flashing antlers are irresistible!)
- Acknowledge that some children find it very to difficult both to look at a person and to listen at the same time, and accept that

CASE STUDY 27

A child who does not make her needs known

Donna is quite happy playing with toys in the pre-school and tends to play alongside or copies other children rather than interacting directly. She doesn't use words but will make sounds and sometimes screams when she cannot get her own way. Donna is still in nappies and makes no effort to indicate that she is wet. She will put equipment straight into her mouth instead of using it for the purpose intended. At snack time, Donna relies upon the adults to give her a drink and biscuit and when confronted with a choice does not express a preference.

Possible reasons for this behaviour:

- Donna has no need to use language since adults anticipate her needs
- Possible physical cause for not producing sounds
- Donna may be at a very early developmental stage and her lack of verbal communication may be a reflection of this

Strategies:

- Donna will need good language role models and the correct use of language modelled by an adult at every opportunity
- Donna will need to be put into situations which require an indication from her about preferences; for example, before art sessions the adult could ask her which brush she would like – 'A big one or a little one?' or 'The red paint or blue paint?' Donna will be expected to either gesture (point) to the item or say the word. The adult should model the word/s clearly, e.g. 'The red paint.' This tactic could be employed throughout the day
- Donna will need to be presented with situations that require her to communicate either verbally or by gesture in non-threatening ways; e.g. at snack times, the adult should present her with a simple choice of fruit or biscuit and expect her to either repeat the word or point to her preference – the adult should then model the word and the built-in reward is the instant giving of the snack
- Donna's lack of speech or an attempt at making speech sounds should never be corrected or greeted with a 'No' – the adult should simply model the word clearly. Neither should Donna be refused anything if she does not say the word

CASE STUDY 28

A child who has no language skills

Jade is just over three years old and does not use any words either at the pre-school or at home. She will indicate her needs by gesturing and pointing but will not attempt to use verbal communication. Although the other children play with Jade, it is becoming increasingly harder for her to join in with them in a meaningful way. She tends, for this reason, to play with the younger children when they are all in the same room. Jade has attended the same pre-school since she was two and the adults have become accustomed to anticipating her needs. Jade has two teenage sisters who had no problems developing language skills.

Possible reasons for this behaviour:

- Jade has become used to being treated as the 'baby' in the family and her parents and big sisters do everything for her so she has no need to use speech at home
- Immaturity – Jade is developing more slowly than her peers and is not at the stage where she is ready to develop speech
- If adults in the pre-school are mirroring the behaviour of the family regarding anticipating need – then Jade has no need to speak in the pre-school
- A physical reason for the lack of speech, e.g. a problem with the tongue, muscles used in speech etc.
- A hearing difficulty

Strategies:

The sensory and physical routes should be explored first by discussing the situation with parents/carers and suggesting an appointment with the GP if this is appropriate. If and when these have been eliminated:
- All adults must stop anticipating Jade's needs but make an effort to spend as much time as possible talking to her
- It would be a good idea if the family could do this with as little distraction as possible, e.g. the television
- An effort should be made by the pre-school and by the family to ask Jade questions requiring more than a 'Yes, No' answer, e.g. 'Do you want juice or milk?' or questions requiring some description, e.g. 'What do you want to play with?'
- Jade may need time to answer
- She may, at first, mispronounce words – this should be greeted with 'Yes, you want the green cup'

- Too many 'What is this?' questions should be avoided – it will become obvious that you do not really want to know the answer – verbal interaction should be as meaningful to Jade as possible. You can attempt this by using everyday situations in the pre-school or home

- Adults should comment on what is happening or on what they are doing with Jade, e.g. if drawing a picture, 'Let's draw a little girl, she has long hair and a red dress on.' And ask questions like, 'What shall we put here?'

- Some ideas for encouraging talking – any games involving talking and watching other people, songs and action rhymes, noisy toys, picture books, cause and effect toys, turn-taking toys, feely toys, pretend play, matching and sorting, anticipation games

- As an interim measure, introduce picture cards to help Jade communicate her choices. (PECS – Picture Exchange Communication System – is widely used in early years settings (**www.pecs-uk.com**))

CASE STUDY 29

A child who uses only single words

Jonathan knows exactly what he wants to do when he comes into the pre-school and will point to the pedal cars and say 'car'. If he is asked about what activity he wants to do in the quiet area he will say 'book'. When asked, at the end of the session, 'Where are you going?' he will say, 'house'. He seems to understand everything and follows instructions but insists upon using only single words to communicate.

Possible reasons for this behaviour:

- Jonathan is quite happy with the way he is communicating and sees no reason to change it
- Since it is always clear what Jonathan wants, adults at home and pre-school have got into the habit of accepting that this is what he is like
- A language delay
- A hearing problem

Strategies:

- Modelling of two- or three-word phrases about what you are doing, e.g. 'Get an apron' or 'Wash your hands'
- At snack time, when Jonathan says 'drink', use an alternative, e.g. give a choice of two things. The adult should then model a two- or three-word phrase, e.g. 'More juice or more milk?'
- It is a good idea to use open questions like 'What do you want?' or 'What is Ben doing?'
- Use familiar rhymes or songs so that Jonathan completes one that you have started and then move on to ordinary sentences for him to complete, e.g. 'Here is Ben's coat and here . . .'; hopefully Jonathan will complete the sentence by adding either '. . . is my coat' or 'here is Jonathan's coat.' This can be done in any situation
- Some ideas for games and activities – acting out pretend games with large toys, asking Jonathan what is happening, using pictures and books and asking what is happening in some of the pictures, games involving giving commands, e.g. 'Touch your nose', involve actions and objects, e.g. 'Jump' or 'Roll ball', turn-taking giving each other commands, e.g. 'teddy eat' or 'baby sleep', hide and seek, and when the toy is found describe where it is, e.g. 'under my chair', 'on the table'

CASE STUDY 30

A child who lacks empathy for others

Charlotte appears not to notice that there are children sitting all around her at story time and she will walk on top of them in order to reach the spot she has chosen to sit. If she wants to play with a particular toy, Charlotte will simply take it from another child and not notice that the child has burst into tears. If an adult points this out, Charlotte will look, without expression, and give the impression that she has not understood or she may giggle. On other occasions, Charlotte will become over-affectionate (especially with adults) and insist on stroking their feet while they tell a story.

Possible reasons for this behaviour:

- A lack of social and play experiences – she may be an only child and not be used to having to consider others
- Charlotte is used to this kind of behaviour and uses it to get what she wants and no one has ever told her to stop
- A sensory impairment – hearing loss and/or visual impairment
- Possible autistic spectrum disorder

Strategies:

- Monitor and observe Charlotte closely, especially in interaction with peers
- Make sure that there are sufficient opportunities for small group teaching of turn-taking games
- Direct teaching of social rules like saying please and thank you and when it is appropriate to laugh and to say sorry
- Ask Charlotte's parent about hearing and eye tests. A sensory assessment may help to decide what the problem is
- If there are major concerns about Charlotte's use of language and understanding of social rules, a referral to a speech and language therapist would help
- Social stories can be used to explore feelings and think about appropriate responses to different situations. Explicit teaching of facial expressions and the vocabulary involved in talking about feelings may also be valuable: 'Was Teddy happy or sad in that story? Let's look at his face. He is smiling, so I think he must be happy. How do we look when we are sad . . . ?'

CASE STUDY 31

A child who fails to carry out instructions

Robert was always described as a mischievous little rogue by pre-school staff. He always had a smile and a glint in his eye. When in the mood he will join in with all activities. Recently he has become more difficult to engage and responds inappropriately when asked to do something. He will either say 'It's silly to do that' or will just continue to do what he wants.

Possible reasons for this behaviour:

- Change of circumstances at home
- Change of circumstances in the pre-school, or he may be outgrowing the present structure of the pre-school
- He may be testing boundaries
- He may be unhappy

Strategies:

- Give Robert responsibilities such as putting the books out
- Check on Robert's progress with the curriculum: is he bored; does he need more challenges?
- Check on structure in the pre-school – could a group of children have specific time for special activities in order to meet their needs regarding the curriculum?
- Give warning time before changing activities and use a visual timetable for the pattern of the day. Encourage Robert to select a certain number of activities that he will do in the session, which are recorded and reviewed at the end of the session
- Discuss the situation with Robert
- Focus very heavily on rewarding Robert whenever he does what he is asked

CASE STUDY 32

A child with poor listening skills

Rowena will sit on the carpet during registration and story time but just moves her head around to look at her peers or to gaze about the room. She needs prompting to answer her name at registration. She finds story times very difficult and can only contribute if asked to point to something in the picture. She can follow nursery routine and will join in when she sees other children doing things.

Possible reasons for this behaviour:

- Language comprehension difficulties
- Anxiety
- Low general cognitive skills
- Hearing difficulties
- Attention difficulties

Strategies:

- Use a highly visual programme so that Rowena is aware of the pattern of the day
- A speech and language assessment may be useful so that a programme can be designed and followed
- An individual programme may be helpful so that Rowena is more secure in what is expected of her
- Use small groups to teach specific tasks and reward Rowena's rate of learning. Her attention difficulties may be reflective of a more generalised difficulty where she will benefit from additional support
- Reward Rowena for all attempts she makes

CASE STUDY 33

A child who remembers little/nothing about stories etc.

Ryan enjoys the big equipment and bikes at pre-school. He is a boisterous boy who attends pre-school every morning. He needs a high level of encouragement to settle at any table-top activity. Story time can be very difficult as Ryan would clearly prefer to be playing elsewhere. Even in a very small group it is difficult to engage Ryan in a story as he finds it difficult to talk about any aspect of the story and says he doesn't know.

Possible reasons for this behaviour:

- Shows no interest in talking activities and would prefer to be playing
- Chooses the big equipment as he finds verbal language difficult
- Does not like to respond in case he is wrong
- Lacks motivation to listen
- Difficulties with listening and attention skills which may reflect a very early developmental stage
- A hearing problem

Strategies:

- Try to involve Ryan in discussion of something he is interested in or try to find books on that area
- Reward Ryan whenever he settles at a task and attempts to listen
- Use a high level of visual and concrete information that can be used in an exploratory way, such as puppets or plays
- Use the big equipment as a reward when Ryan has completed a listening activity
- Use strategies and games to develop short-term memory (see Section 1 and Top tips)

CASE STUDY 34

A child who is hurtful to others

Thomas has been in the nursery for two years and has always been a bit of a 'loner'. However, he has recently started saying unkind and tactless remarks to adults and pupils, using phrases that are inappropriately adult. Some other children have become upset at the personal remarks but Thomas has shown no understanding that his words have been the cause and has refused to apologise for calling people fat and ugly. He has recently started making insulting and upsetting comments about other children's families such as 'Your mummy is going to die.'

Possible reasons for this behaviour:

- Has experience of inappropriate role models
- Has had such remarks made to him
- Has received a lot of attention when told off for making unkind remarks
- Has a social communication difficulty and is unable to empathise with others

Strategies:

- Tactically ignore hurtful comments whenever possible and praise children who cope well with Thomas's remarks
- Use circle time and stories to emphasise the need to be kind
- Raise the problem with his parents to ensure that he is not being exposed to inappropriate role models at home, e.g. elder brother/sister and their friends
- Have definite consequences for upsetting others, e.g. apologising and having a target of saying kind things to others
- Rehearsing what are acceptable things to say – even if Thomas does not understand the reason behind this, it will help him socially

CASE STUDY 35

A child who is able to count by rote very well but appears to have no understanding

Lewis loves numbers and is able to recognise numbers to 100. He can count to 100 without making a mistake and loves to perform this task for anyone who will listen. He will point out numbers on clocks and in pictures or indeed anywhere else he sees them. However, when asked to count a number of objects, Lewis does not have one-to-one correspondence and will miscount. If asked to say who has more, e.g. 'If Peter has two sweets and Tom has one – who has more?', Lewis appears not to understand and will sometimes just repeat the last word he has heard. Lewis cannot carry out instructions like 'Find seven cars.' Lewis does not really show much interest in anything else apart from numbers.

Possible reasons for this behaviour:

- Lewis has a very good visual memory and an interest in numerals
- His memory skills are in advance of his general development in learning
- If there are other significant behaviours – there may be a possibility of a social and communication disorder

Strategies:

- Observe Lewis closely and work with him on a one-to-one basis to ascertain exactly what he does and does not understand about counting and the value of numbers. For example, if he appears not to understand the value of even very small numbers, start with the number 1, use real objects to show 1 teddy, 1 car and so on. Make sure you do this in a variety of contexts. Move onto the number 2 when 1 is secure but continue to use real objects and try to relate these to his own experiences
- Begin one-to-one correspondence by choosing very small numbers of real objects, e.g. cars
- Model the method by showing how you point to (or even touch) the car as you say 'One, Two.'
- Take Lewis' hand and show him how to do this, repeating (and asking him to join in) 'One, Two.' Gradually increase the number of objects when you are sure this is secure
- You may then be able to move on to things like finding a specific number of objects, first from 1–5 and then 1–10
- You could bring counting into everything you do, using every opportunity, e.g. 'Lewis drew two pictures today' – and hold up two drawings as the visual reinforcement

CASE STUDY 36

A child who doesn't recognise basic shapes and cannot match same shapes

Shane is a friendly boy who rushes into pre-school every Monday. He is due to transfer to a mainstream school in a few weeks and is in the transition group. All the other children in that group now recognise many shapes and can name them and make patterns with them. Shane is the only group member who cannot recognise basic shapes or even match them.

Possible reasons for this behaviour:

- Lower cognitive skills generally
- Lack of interest in adult-led tasks
- Language difficulties

Strategies:

- Many children's early difficulties with mathematical development are the result of poor language skills. It may be most helpful to focus on language skills in more meaningful contexts initially and then return to specific mathematical concepts
- Use shapes that have meaning for the child and talk about the shapes, e.g. shape sorter posting box which is dependent on matching shapes. Concrete examples that are fun to use are often the most effective way of engaging such children
- Go outside on walks if possible and look for shapes in nature and on buildings or structures like roads, gates, walls etc.

SECTION 3

Planning

- The Code of Practice
- The planning cycle
- Observation
- Writing a programme
- Setting targets
- Individual Education Plans

The Code of Practice

Early years settings must have regard to the Code of Practice for Special Educational Needs (**www.dfes.gov.uk**). This relates to children with significant difficulties who need support which is 'different from and additional to' the differentiated curriculum plan that is in place as part of normal provision.

In the early years it can sometimes be difficult to assess whether or not to write an Individual Education Plan (IEP) for a child. For some children, there will be no doubt that they should be included on your Special Needs Register and you will have to provide some extra support and intervention for them. This support may be in the form of an IEP, extra equipment or one-to-one assistance. The action decided upon should in any case be individualised so the child is enabled to make progress. A child with profound and complex learning difficulties will require careful assessment and an individualised programme. For others, though, it is less clear cut. Very young children mature at different rates and the so-called 'norm' includes a wide range of abilities and behaviours. Careful observations and consultation with parents, and your Area SENCO if necessary, will help you to make the best possible provision.

Referring to the Definition of Special Educational Needs in the Code of Practice can help. It says:

Children have a learning difficulty if they:
a. have a significantly greater difficulty in learning than the majority of children of the same age; or
b. have a disability which prevents or hinders them from making use of educational facilities of a kind generally provided for children of the same age in schools within the area of the local education authority
c. are under compulsory school age and fall within the definition at a. or b. above or would so do if special educational provision was not made for them.

Children must not be regarded as having a learning difficulty solely because the language or form of language of their home is different from the language in which they will be taught.
Special educational provision means:
a. for children of two or over, educational provision which is additional to or different from, the educational provision made generally for child of their age in schools maintained by the LEA, other than special schools, in the area.
b. for children under two, educational provision of any kind.

Although the word 'significantly' is open to interpretation, it does help to differentiate children who may have a slight delay in learning or are immature from the child experiencing real problems. There will always be a number of children in pre-school settings, however, who will benefit from extra support and consideration. They may not qualify for extra resources and funding, but they are still 'vulnerable' and early years settings can do a lot to minimise or remove barriers to learning for these children.

There are many children in pre-schools, for example, who are receiving speech and language therapy. This can range from children with simple speech sounds difficulties to children with severe language difficulties. It is important to take great care in the planning for these children. Children with problems pronouncing sounds like 'c' and 't' can often be planned for in the general curriculum plan. You may have several children like this and rather than writing IEPs for them, you will be meeting their needs by planning activities for groups focused on their particular needs. Although technically they may be receiving outside agency help, careful consideration should be given to whether their needs are significant enough to be registered at Action Plus. (Refer to the Definition of Special Educational Needs in your Code of Practice and assess whether the difficulty is impacting upon the ability to access the curriculum.) Indeed, you may have a large number of children with phonology problems and if this is simply a case of not pronouncing the odd sound (usually c, t, and d) then it would not make sense to add them all to your Special Needs Register. However, it is very important to monitor this closely so that the difficulty does not persist and impact on the child's ability to hear and make sounds and to eventually develop reading skills. For children who have difficulty with processing language, the picture is different. They certainly need to be assessed by a speech and language therapist and may need planning which includes writing an Individual Education Plan. If you are in any doubt, you may wish to enlist advice from your Area Special Needs Co-ordinator.

The planning cycle

Children's needs must be at the heart of the planning cycle. An ongoing process of observation and review will enable early years practitioners to maximise the opportunities for all children, including those with special needs.

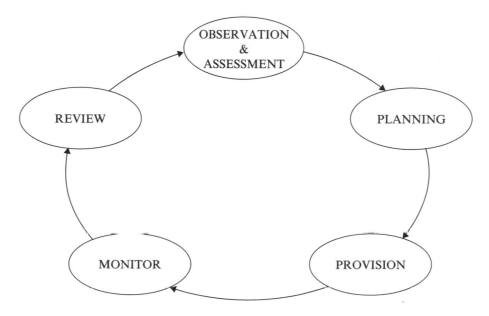

Observation

The process of observing children is an integral part of early years provision. You need to ask:

- How should we be observing?
- Who should be doing the observing?
- Where should we be doing observations?
- How should we record observations?

By observing a child you will gather important information about his strengths and interests, areas for development, reviewing provision, forward planning and reporting. Careful observation will help to assess knowledge, skills, understanding and attitudes. In the absence of observations, it is very easy to make assumptions about children. There may be specific reasons for doing observations – for example, to gather information about certain behaviours like interaction skills or behaviours causing concern. Observing for a purpose gives the practitioner factual evidence to inform planning or reporting.

How should we be observing?

Observations should be as objective as possible. An observation is more useful if it is factual and as free as possible from opinions. It is also very important to record what has actually been SEEN rather than recording what we THINK we have seen. 'What we look for is what we see' is an old saying but is a warning to all those working with children to place importance not on what we WANT to see but on what we actually SEE.

The use of language when recording observations is important. Making a statement like 'Andrew was slow to complete the puzzle', is an opinion without any supporting evidence. Compare it to 'Andrew took 10 minutes to do a 12-piece puzzle.' The second statement is simply a statement of fact and tells us exactly how long Andrew took to do the puzzle on that particular day. It would be unfair to base any planning on this isolated observation. It may be that Andrew is usually good at puzzles but was not feeling well or didn't want to do the puzzle at that particular time. Judgemental language may have the effect of lowering the expectations of people working with the child. Phrases like 'lacks confidence', 'poor motor skills', 'has difficulty listening and concentrating' are often not backed up with evidence and do not give you the information you need to plan the next step. If the statement said something like 'Sophie is able to drink out of a beaker with a lid with some adult support; if given an open beaker, she misses her mouth and spills the drink', this tells you not only that Sophie has poor motor co-ordination but also something about her developmental stage. Observations may never be entirely free from judgemental statements but an awareness of this helps the observer to be as accurate as possible.

There are many different ways in which observations are made. If you are in the habit of carrying a notepad with you at all times, quick observations and notes can be made as part of the usual working pattern of the day. This is a good way of getting information down when it is fresh in your mind. Making brief notes like this comes with practice and often, the less you write, the more meaningful and to the point it is and the more it can convey. Some practitioners like to use 'Post It' notes. Observations like this are incidental and unplanned and help to build a developing picture of the child. For example, you may overhear a conversation between two children along the lines of, 'I want that crayon, they're my crayons' says Joe to Liam as Liam attempts to select a crayon from the box on the table. Liam replies, 'We have to share the crayons, Joe, put them back in the box then we can take them when we need them, look, I'm doing it.' It is worth noting this exchange in regard to Liam as it tells us a great deal about how he is developing. (I observed this in one of the pre-schools I support; it made my day because I had been supporting this setting with some challenging children and it represented a huge step forward for Liam.)

Who should be doing the observing?

The whole team should be involved in observing children. Some staff members may need support at first but the more people involved in observing, the more varied the information will be. It also helps to build a more rounded picture of a child and in turn will help to focus the planning more effectively. Some settings ask for observations to be carried out by their Area SENCO, Health Visitor or other professional. Parental permission should always be sought. Formal observations of this kind can be useful in planning an effective programme. However, informal observations by an outside agency and a discussion with key workers can also be a very good way forward. If the child knows he is being 'observed' it really negates the point of the exercise.

Parents can also contribute to the observing process. They hold important information about their child which can be useful to the practitioner. It is important to be sensitive about involving parents and to know who is interested in becoming involved in this process and to what degree. Pre-school practitioners are traditionally good at parent liaison because the setting and parents are used to ongoing informal and formal liaison procedures.

It is important to observe over the whole range of activities and especially during play. It is worth considering using different types of observation in order to build a well-rounded picture of a child's abilities.

Participatory and non-participatory observation

All practitioners are involved in this type of observation as part of their everyday work. Whilst engaged in an activity with a group of children, you may hear something you wish to record. If you wait until the session is over to record what you have seen or heard, it is easy to forget exactly what has happened. This is where carrying a notepad in your pocket comes into its own – a brief word or phrase is enough to jog your memory and make your recording much more accurate.

Non-participatory observation is when the observer takes no part in the task but observes one particular child for a period of time. It is important to be seated at a distance that allows you to hear exchanges taking place but not too near to be affecting what is going on. The children will need to know that you are not available to help while you are observing. Settings have their own ways of dealing with this; some observers wear something special on their heads or a badge. It does not really matter as long as everyone knows what it means.

Time sampling

This is when a practitioner observes a particular child at specified time intervals. For example, observes a particular child every 10 minutes. Or observes a group of children in the same way. An area of the setting may be the focus of the observation, for example the writing area. The observations might include who is using the equipment, are they using it independently, with adult support, what is being said? This kind of observation can tell you about children and about the value of resources.

Frequency sampling

This type of observation targets particular behaviours and how many times they occur. For example, if concerns are raised about the interaction skills of a particular child, observations may include how many interactions took place over a specified period, if the child initiated the interaction and how many times, if the child used different areas of the pre-school, if the child interacted with adults and children.

Recording and storing observations

Some settings are lucky enough to have purpose-built rooms with office and storage space. However, not everyone has access to these facilities. Where there is limited space or the setting has to hire rooms for the duration of their sessions, storing equipment and files can be a problem. The paperwork relating to children attending the pre-school may contain sensitive information. It is important to make sure that there is a safe place to store such information. A simple envelope file for each child is a quick and easy way to keep all the information together. Most settings have their own method of keeping records. It is important to remember that it is the quality of the recording that is important and not the quantity. For example, volumes of observations that record 'Johnny played in the sand, then the sticking, then the cars, then the climbing frame etc.' may not be very useful to the next practitioner, whilst a focused observation recording 'In the space of 15 minutes, during story time, Johnny initiated aggression towards his peers 13 times' can tell the practitioner a great deal. (See Appendix 1 for example observation format and an example of an observation.)

Writing a programme

Once information has been gathered and assessments have been made, the next step in the cycle is planning a programme. Key staff and, if possible, parents need to be involved. It is the role of the Special Needs Co-ordinator to ensure that this happens. It may be that, at the beginning, the SENCO takes the lead in this but as staff become more confident, they will be able to do this without the presence of the SENCO. Obviously, the SENCO will know that this is taking place and will oversee and support the entire process. A lot of information will have been gathered and a sense of the child's areas of difficulty will be clearly understood. Information may have come from outside agencies and this will add further information for practitioners involved in the planning process.

Sometimes a child may present with complex difficulties, say for example a child who is suffering from cerebral palsy. In these cases things can appear to be overwhelming and it is possible to feel that you do not know where to start. For instance, with so many areas to develop, which do you choose? Good observations can help. Usually, self-help skills are a good place to start. Staff closely involved with a particular child will have a good idea about areas for development. Choose the most pressing difficulty, the most needed skill for independence to work on first.

The SENCO, the parents and key worker should be involved in planning an appropriate programme, but the child himself should also be involved in the process as much as is possible. Older children benefit a great deal from this and even young children can be included by using appropriate explanations about any change in interventions.

The Code of Practice outlines two stages for planning:

Early Years Action and
Early Years Action Plus

Triggers for intervention through Early Years Action could be the practitioner's or parent's concern about a child who despite receiving appropriate early education experiences:

- Makes little or no progress when teaching approaches are particularly targeted to improve the child's identified area of weakness
- Continues working at levels significantly below those expected for children of a similar age in certain areas
- Presents persistent emotional and/or behavioural difficulties, which are not ameliorated by the behaviour management techniques usually employed in the setting
- Has sensory or physical problems and continues to make little or no progress despite the provision of personal aids and equipment
- Has communication and/or interaction difficulties and requires specific individual interventions in order to access learning

Early Years Action – the child has an Individual Education Plan. The setting is able to meet the needs of the child by providing a programme which is different from and additional to the general curriculum plan in place already.

Triggers for seeking help from external agencies: despite receiving an individualised programme and/or concentrated support the child:

- Continues to make little or no progress in specific areas over a long period of time
- Continues working at an early years curriculum substantially below that expected of children of the same age
- Has emotional or behavioural difficulties which substantially and regularly interfere with the child's own learning or that of the group, despite having an individualised behaviour management programme

Early Years Action Plus – the child has an Individual Education Plan. The setting is able to meet the needs of the child by providing a programme which is different from and additional to the general curriculum plan in place already – with the ongoing support of external agencies.

Setting targets

When information has been gathered, the SENCO, the parents (if possible) and the key worker(s) will decide upon the course of action. If it is decided that an IEP (Individual Education Plan) should be written, the targets need to be fully discussed. The targets need to be SMART:

- **S**pecific
- **M**easureable
- **A**chieveable
- **R**ealistic
- **T**imescaled

Writing targets should be differentiated from long-term aims. It is useful to think of the long-term aim and then to break this down to form small-steps targets which are to be worked on with the child over a specified period of time.

The 'formula' for writing targets:

What do you want the child to do?
Under what circumstances?
To what degree of success?

An example:

Freddy will be able to pick out his name card from a choice of two every time he is asked
What do you want the child to do – pick his name card out
Under what circumstances – from a choice of two
To what degree of success – every time or 100%

A further example:

Freddy will be able to point to his name card with adult support two out of every three times he is asked

In the first example, it looks as though Freddy has already worked on the example quoted in 'further example'. The same 'formula' has been used to write the target but the stage of development is different. The long-term aim for Freddy might be to develop early or pre-literacy skills.

INDIVIDUAL EDUCATION PLAN

NAME: *Donna*   **DoB:**   **PRE-SCHOOL:**

PLAN NO: **ACTION/ACTION PLUS DATE:**

AREA(S) FOR DEVELOPMENT: *Speech and language*

TARGETS	STRATEGIES, RESOURCES, CONTRIBUTIONS
1 *Donna will be able to make her choice clear to an adult when presented with two items to choose from. She will do this every time.*	*Donna will be offered a choice of two things (biscuit or fruit, crayon or brush etc.) and will be expected to indicate by gesture at first.* *An adult will model the correct word.* *Adults will not anticipate.*
2 *Donna will be able to copy a word modelled by an adult – 'mummy', 'daddy', 'Donna'.*	*Adults should model the word whenever appropriate and change them as Donna becomes confident, always choosing words that have personal meaning for her.*
3 *Donna will be able to name a toy she wishes to play with at least two out of three times.*	*Use favourite toys and model the correct name – encourage Donna to copy the word – if she gestures or makes even a slight attempt she should be given the toy.*

TO BE ACHIEVED BY: **REVIEW DATE:**

SIGNATURES: **SENCO:**   **PARENTS/GUARDIANS:**

REVIEW
1
2
3

FUTURE ACTION

SIGNATURES: **SENCO:**   **PARENTS/GUARDIANS:**

INDIVIDUAL EDUCATION PLAN

NAME: *Harrison* **DoB:**   **PRE-SCHOOL:**

PLAN NO: **ACTION/ACTION PLUS DATE:**

AREA(S) FOR DEVELOPMENT: *Personal and social – independence, self-help skills*

TARGETS	STRATEGIES, RESOURCES, CONTRIBUTIONS
1 *Harrison will be able to get his own apron for painting and be able to put it on by himself.*	*Adults should use prompts at first but not help directly, even if the apron is not on properly.*
2 *Harrison will be able to find his coat at home time and be able to put it on by himself.*	*Adults should use prompts and verbal instructions and only assist by using minimal interventions – withdrawing these gradually.*
3 *Harrison will be the helper at snack time, assisting an adult by offering children their snacks and pouring drinks.*	*Harrison will need to practise pouring water from a jug into a container and may need adult prompting, encouraging him to distribute snacks to children, perhaps even offering them a choice.*

TO BE ACHIEVED BY: **REVIEW DATE:**

SIGNATURES: **SENCO:**   **PARENTS/GUARDIANS:**

REVIEW

1

2

3

FUTURE ACTION

SIGNATURES: **SENCO:**   **PARENTS/GUARDIANS:**

Reviewing and monitoring IEPs

The Code of Practice states that IEPs should be reviewed regularly and at least three times a year. However, it is useful for settings to keep IEPs under review continually. Reviews should be held at manageable intervals and ideally should include parents' views. The meetings need not be unduly formal. In the case of children with complex needs, it may be a good idea to have a set meeting that could include external professionals. In this case, the meeting may be viewed as more formal and be intimidating for parents. Early years settings have traditionally had very good relationships with parents and will be able to do much to make this as comfortable as possible.

Now that we are living in a climate of accountability, it may be desirable (and useful) to implement some sort of monitoring system. Every time the IEP is worked on, it may be useful to record this BRIEFLY in some way. The tracking sheet in the recording pack in Appendix 1 may be useful for doing this. The date and a one-word comment is all that is needed to show progress (or the lack of it) and also the number of times targets have been worked on over a period of time. This brief record could be used to inform further planning.

SECTION 4

Top tips for teaching and learning

Story time

Tidy-up time

Moving around the setting

Developing attention and listening skills

Inclusion – making learning accessible to all children

Outdoor play

Encouraging turn-taking

Encouraging children to follow instructions

Encouraging memory skills

Teaching children with hearing impairment

Teaching children with visual impairment

Top tips for story time

- Show the children the front cover of the book, ask what the story might be about to create interest – if you are really interested, they will be too

- Be well prepared and have other books on hand in case you have more time than planned

- Use a big book if possible so that children at the back of the group can see

- Make use of visual aids like puppets and/or story sacks with the characters in the story so that children can act out the story as it is being told

- If you have spare copies of the book – give them out to children who have difficulty concentrating so they can follow the story more easily

- Involve the children in the story, make it an interactive experience by asking children to listen out for things, stop to ask questions about what they think might happen next etc.

- Vary your tone of voice – if you are interested in the story telling, the children will be interested and will listen

- If you have large groups, split into two smaller groups for story if possible

- Use a space which is conducive to sitting comfortably without too many distractions – screen the story-telling corner off from the rest of the room if possible

Top tips for 'tidy-up time'

- Adults should model the appropriate behaviour

- Everything should be labelled with a picture and a word to help children to be independent

- Children should be warned when it is nearly time to tidy up

- A signal like a rainstick might be an alternative to an adult telling the children they should tidy up

- Children will become aware of where and how equipment is stored during these sessions; some children will need to be shown how to put things away at first

- EXPECT children to do the tidying – even very young children are capable of putting toys into a box (it doesn't matter if the tidy-up period takes a long time at first)

Top tips for moving around the setting

- Consider if it is absolutely necessary to line children up when moving from room to room

- Consider whether it is necessary for the whole group to have to move at the same time

- When lining up, consider using the time involved for teaching basic concepts like the use of positional language, colour, sounds, size etc., e.g. 'make a line if you are wearing anything blue' or 'if your house number has the number 3 in it'

- Anticipate the children who may find lining up difficult and engage them by supporting them closely at first and not letting these times take any longer than necessary

- Give those children specific jobs to do, e.g. holding the door open

- Do not let children fail by not examining your own practice first – small changes to everyday events like routine lining up can make a big difference to a child who sees no point in these things in the first place

- When introducing new activities, always SHOW the children HOW you would like them to do it – model the correct way of behaving and/or choose a child to do it as a demonstration – just telling them will not always have the same effect

- On outings, consider using a rope for children to hold if walking along pavements

Top tips for developing attention and listening skills

In whole groups:

- Encourage children to look at you when you are speaking
- Use simple language to describe what you are doing as you play
- Have a well-rehearsed routine for things like story time
- Do not take too long to get started – as soon as the story or activity looks interesting, most children will listen
- Don't worry unduly if one or two children take a long time to settle or do not join the group – if what you are doing is interesting they will become attentive
- If you give them attention instead of the children who ARE listening you are giving out mixed messages
- Ask questions about the text/activity
- Praise children who are demonstrating good listening skills
- If children find it hard to sit still for the entire session – direct them to another activity so that it is adult led and not child led (examine how long you expect children to sit still for and tailor your story session accordingly)
- Use signals like rainsticks, turning the light off and on again etc. for gaining attention and vary it so that children become sensitive to these different stimuli and their interest is maintained
- Use a sound like a new musical instrument and play it at various intervals to see who can hear it/identify it – tell the children you will be doing it at the beginning of the session
- Play games like Chinese whispers
- When engaged in a listening activity – make sure there are no distractions going on or eye-catching toys out
- Make an assortment of shakers, drums and danglers filled with a variety of things like rice, lentils, buttons or small pebbles. Explore the differing sounds when struck with a variety of objects
- Have a selection of shakers filled with different things (see above). Give children one of each and see if they can match the sound after you have played one of the shakers
- Have a selection of instruments. Play two different instruments, one after the other. Can the children copy in the correct order?
- For older children – ask them to close their eyes while you play one of the instruments and see if the children can tell you which one was played
- For very small groups – clap hands, tap fingers or stamp feet. Ask the children to copy the rhythm

In one-to-one or small groups:

- Use the child/children's special interests

- Make sure that children are looking at you – you may need to position yourself at child level

- Play games that require very close listening skills, e.g. sound lotto

- Expect children to concentrate for very short periods at first and gradually increase the time span

- Anticipate the child's attention span and direct him to another activity BEFORE he becomes unsettled so that it is adult led and not child led

- If engaging in table-top activities, consider relocating to the floor using large cushions so the child with physical and/or medical difficulties can join in

- If using writing or drawing materials, have a variety of sizes of pencils, brushes, crayons available

- Have different colours of paper available for children with visual difficulties

- Find stories with characters who are disabled and discuss this with the children

- Remember to have fun

Top tips for inclusion – making learning accessible to all children

- If using persona dolls, have some who wear glasses, use a wheelchair or a hearing aid etc.

- Be careful about the materials equipment is made from to minimise any potential allergic reactions

- Involve visually impaired children in any changes you make to the setting or where the equipment is stored

- Put colour into water trays and/or use colour whenever using water for measuring

- Add scent to water

- Make sure you provide a wide variety of equipment and musical instruments, e.g. vibrating instruments are useful for children with visual and hearing difficulties

- Use the purest play sand if you have children with conditions like eczema

- Have gloves on hand if some children are especially allergic to some materials

- Vary the temperature of the water

- Use different textured materials for making displays, models etc.

- Use dried peas or pasta shapes for weighing instead of sand

Top tips for outdoor play

- Have a variety of pedal cars, bikes and tricycles of differing sizes available and stick velcro to handlebars and pedals

- Make sure there is adequate adult help available to support children with sensory or physical/medical difficulties

- Have a variety of pushchairs in different sizes – some children with co-ordination problems find these useful as walking aids as well as enjoying just playing with them

- Use a variety of seating outdoors – some children with heightened sensitivity may prefer to sit on large bean bags or hard wooden chairs

- Consider the use of equipment that allows for deep pressure, e.g. trampolines, sit and bounce balls or space hoppers, body rolling games, large saucers for twirling children around, tactile games using finger paints, shaving foam etc.

- Think about use of space to encourage digging

Top tips for encouraging turn-taking

- Make sure there are no unnecessary distractions

- Use simple language, e.g. 'my turn', 'your turn'

- Use facial expression, gesture and/or signs to encourage interest

- Demonstrate the activity at first so that children understand what you expect

- Play hiding games – hide three or four toys, ask for a specific one. Children should find the one you have asked for and not the others

- Cover well-known objects with a cloth. Give the children clues about the objects and see if they can guess what they are

Top tips for encouraging children to follow instructions

- Play games like 'follow my leader' and 'simple Simon'

- Allow children to watch while you perform tasks such as cleaning and tidying – children learn through observation

Top tips for encouraging memory skills

- Kim's game – place three–six objects on a table and ask the child to look at them. Take one object away while the child covers his eyes and ask him to name the missing object. Alternatively, cover the objects and ask him if he can remember them all

- Coloured towers – place three or more coloured bricks inside a tube (kitchen roll middle), see if the child can remember the sequence and copy in his tube

- Remembering objects – place three objects or pictures in front of the child and let him look for a while. Remove the objects and silently count to 10. Can the child remember the objects and the order they were in?

- Copy me – act out an action, e.g. clapping, hopping. Ask the child to copy you. Add another action, see if the child can copy

Top tips for teaching children with hearing impairment

- Keep background noise to a minimum
- Be close to the child you are speaking to – not more than three feet away
- Accept attempts at speech positively and give the correct pattern
- Repeat language more often than you think it necessary
- Slightly emphasise the key word
- Do NOT correct the child's speech
- Try to put yourself at child level
- If addressing the group – position the hearing impaired child at the front and to one side of the group
- Use a good voice level – not too quiet
- If checking for comprehension – do not say 'did you hear me?'
- Use visual aids
- Make sure the child can see your face – be careful about shadows or having your back to a bright window

Top tips for teaching children with visual impairment

- Encourage participation in activities by the use of different textured resources

- Use different coloured paper for activities like painting – it is easier for some children to see marks made on yellow or grey paper, for example

- Invest in or borrow toys that make different sounds

- Use musical instruments

- Encourage the child to become familiar with his environment by making sure that he knows where the toilets are and can find his own way there when he feels confident

- Use textured 'markers' around doorways and walkways

- If you move things around the setting – make sure you tell the child and allow him to explore the new arrangement

- Help the child to be independent by giving practice at self-help skills like dressing and managing eating and drinking

- Involve his other senses, e.g. use scent, flowers with scents, use different textures whenever possible, think about equipment and instruments which make interesting sounds etc.

APPENDIX 1

Recording pack

SEN Register

Observation sheet

Observation sheet example

IEP – front of file detail

IEP blank

IEP tracking sheet

Meeting with parents/carers

Special Educational Needs Register

Pre-school:	SENCO:
Date:	

Child's name	DoB	Stage	Key worker	Date added to register

OBSERVATION SHEET

NAME: **DoB:**   **DATE:**

PRE-SCHOOL:

REASON FOR OBSERVATION:

TIME:	OBSERVATIONS: record the context of the behaviour (the activity going on, people present etc.), the possible trigger for the behaviour (what happened immediately before), the exact behaviour itself – just as it happened (what you saw, not what you think about it).	INITIALS

ACTION:

OBSERVATION SHEET

NAME: Sam Marshall	DoB: 24.06.2000	DATE: 20.05.04

PRE-SCHOOL: Lark Lane

REASON FOR OBSERVATION: High dependency on adults

TIME:	OBSERVATIONS: record the context of the behaviour (the activity going on, people present etc.), the possible trigger for the behaviour (what happened immediately before), the exact behaviour itself – just as it happened (what you saw, not what you think about it).	INITIALS
9.30	Sam arrives with Mum and she takes off his coat and hangs it up, helps him to change his shoes and leads him by the hand into nursery.	AG
10.45	Sam has been playing in the water without an apron on - he is soaking wet but doesn't say anything to anyone. At snack time, KL asks him if he wants to change his clothes and he says 'yes'. She takes him into the home corner to change his top. He stands and waits for her to take off his top. KL hands him a clean T-shirt and says 'Put this on'. Sam takes some time getting it over his head - and ends up with it on back-to-front. KL takes it off again and puts it on the right way round.	AG
11.00	Most children put on a jacket to go outside but Sam does not bother. He asks KL to help him change his shoes. She is helping Katy and suggests Sam tries himself - he sits and waits for her to come.	AG
Action	Speak to Sam's mum about encouraging him to do things by himself. At nursery, set him one new task every week to complete by himself - changing his shoes, putting on his coat, tidying away the Lego etc. and praise him for his efforts. Start a star chart for this. Put Sam in charge of the fruit plate at snack time - handing round pieces of fruit to everyone in the group. Praise him for helping out. Review in 3 weeks' time.	

INDIVIDUAL EDUCATION PLAN – FRONT OF FILE DETAIL

NAME:	**DoB:**	**PRE-SCHOOL:**
ADMISSION DATE:	**ACTION/ACTION PLUS:**	
DATE:		

AREA(S) FOR DEVELOPEMENT:

LEARNING	**BEHAVIOUR/ EMOTIONAL**	**PHYSICAL/ SENSORY**

Detail:

SUPPORT DETAILS – INVOLVEMENT OF OUTSIDE AGENCIES:

PASTORAL CARE/MEDICAL REQUIREMENTS:

SPECIALIST PROGRAMMES/RESOURCES REQUIRED:

PARENTAL SUPPORT/INVOLVEMENT:

MONITORING AND REVIEW ARRANGEMENTS/FREQUENCY OF MEETINGS:

INDIVIDUAL EDUCATION PLAN

NAME: DoB: PRE-SCHOOL:

PLAN NO: ACTION/ACTION PLUS DATE:

AREA(S) FOR DEVELOPMENT:

TARGETS	STRATEGIES, RESOURCES, CONTRIBUTIONS
1	
2	
3	

TO BE ACHIEVED BY: REVIEW DATE:
SIGNATURES: SENCO: PARENTS/GUARDIANS:

REVIEW
1
2
3

FUTURE ACTION

SIGNATURES: SENCO: PARENTS/GUARDIANS:

INDIVIDUAL EDUCATION PLAN – TRACKING SHEET

NAME: **DoB:**   **DATE:**

KEY WORKER: **PRE-SCHOOL:**

DATE:	TARGET: (1, 2, OR 3)	COMMENTS:	DATE ACHIEVED:

MEETING WITH PARENTS/CARERS

Pre-school: **Date:**

Name of child:

Key worker:

Parent/carer:

Points discussed

Action

Signatures: Parent/carer: Key worker:

APPENDIX 2

Developmental checklists

Cognition

Expressive language development

Acquisition of speech sounds

It is important that any checklist be used with sensitivity. It should not be used to highlight what a child cannot do or to create unrealistic expectations. Instead, it should be seen as a very rough guide to the development steps most children take between the ages specified.

Cognition
(compiled using various sources)

Age 2–3 years

- Finds specific book on request

- Names common objects

- Completes 3-piece jigsaw

- Imitates when a vertical and horizontal line is drawn

- Copies a circle

- Matches 3 colours

- Matches textures

- Points to big, little on request

- Places objects in, on and under on request

- Names objects that make sounds

- Puts together 4-part nesting toy

- Stacks 5 or more rings on a peg in order

- Names actions

Age 3–4 years

- Names big and little objects

- Points to 10 body parts on request

- Points to boy and girl on request

- Tells if object is heavy or light

- Tells what happens next in simple repetitive story

- Matches 1 to 1 (3 or more objects)

- Points to long and short

- Tells which objects go together

- Draws V shape in imitation and is able to copy series of V strokes

- Arranges objects into categories

- Counts to 10 objects in imitation

- Adds leg/arm to incomplete man

- Completes 6-piece puzzle without errors

- Knows same and different

- Names 3 colours on request

- Names 3 shapes on request

Age 4–5 years

- Picks up to 15 objects on request

- Names 5 textures

- Recalls 4 objects seen in a picture

- Copies triangle on request

- Repeats familiar rhymes

- Tells whether objects are heavy or light

- Tells what is missing when 1 object is removed from a group of 3

- Names 8 colours

- Names 3 common coins

- Matches symbols (letters and numerals)

- Tells colour of named objects

- Retells 5 main facts from story heard 3 times

- Draws man (head, trunk, 4 limbs)

- Sings 5 lines of a song

- Imitates pyramid of 10 blocks

- Names long and short

- Places object behind, next to, beside

- Matches equal sets to sample of 1 to 10 objects

- Counts by rote to 20

- Names first, middle and last position

Expressive language development
(compiled from various sources)

3 years (plus)

- Using 4 + words together e.g. mummy me go shops

- Grammar continues to develop

- Beginning to use longer sentences

- Asking many different questions

4–5 years

- Vocabulary developing well

- Able to talk using more abstract vocabulary and topics

- Use of concept names continues to develop

  - Shapes

  - Sizes

  - Comparatives

  - Adverbs

- Pronouns used more appropriately

- Developing the skills of summarising the content of stories

- Able to describe a sequence of events

- Able to talk about recent events and experiences

- Initiates conversation – asks questions, makes requests etc.

Acquisition of speech sounds (age at which 90% of children have acquired the sound)

Age 2–3 years

- m, n, p, b, t, d, w, ng, k, g, h

May use the following:

- Reduplication – babababa

- Consonant harmony – gog (dog)

- Final consonant deletion – ca (cat)

- Cluster reduction – poon (spoon)

- Fronting – dirl (girl)

- Stopping – dun (sun)

- Gliding – yoyi (lolly)

Age 3 years

All above sounds for previous age group plus:

- f, s, y, l

May use:

- 'th' said as 'f'

- 'r' said as 'w'

Age 3–4 years

All of the above sounds plus:

- z, ch, j, r, sh

- Child begins to say clusters, child is no longer stopping or fronting, child is saying the ends of words

Age 4 years onwards

- th, zh

GLOSSARY

autistic spectrum disorder (ASD)   a developmental disorder that is characterised by social and communication difficulties

cognition   how a child thinks and learns

dyspraxia   motor co-ordination disorder

emotional development   the way a child controls and expresses his feelings

expressive language   spoken language, talking

global development delay   non-specific learning difficulties

language delay   limited and/or immature use of language

language disorder   a difficulty with the understanding of words and their use

neurological   to do with the brain and nervous system

phonology   speech sounds system

receptive language   understanding what is said to you

self-esteem   the way we see ourselves. A child with good self-esteem has a positive picture of himself

social   the way a child relates to his peers and adults and how he is able to respond to systems and organisation

social awareness   the ability to act in an appropriate way in different settings, such as organised groups like pre-school settings

speech disorder   this could be a difficulty with pronouncing single or combined sounds and/or sentence structure

structure   giving structure to an activity or a day's activities means planning and organising things to good effect

REFERENCES

DfES (2001) *Special Educational Needs Code of Practice.*

DfES (2001) *SEN Toolkit.*

Hohmann, M.N. and Weikart, D.P. (1995) *Educating Young Children: Active Learning Practices for Preschool and Childcare Programmes.* Ypsilanti, MI: High/Scope Press.

FURTHER READING

Drifte, Collette (2003) *Handbook for Pre-School SEN Provision*. London: David Fulton Publishers.

Evans, L. and East, V. (2001) *At a Glance: A Quick Guide to Children's Special Educational Needs*. Birmingham: Questions Publishing.

Glenn, A., Cousins, J. and Helps, A. (2004) *Behaviour in the Early Years*. London: David Fulton Publishers.

Mortimer, H. (2002) *Special Needs Handbook*. Leamington Spa: Scholastic.

Nash, Marion, Lowe, Jackie and Tracey Palmer (2003) *Spirals Series: Language Development: Circle Time Sessions to Improve Communication Skills*. London: David Fulton Publishers.

USEFUL ADDRESSES

National Autistic Society
393 City Road
London EC1V 1NG
Tel: 020 7833 2299
Email: nas@nas.org.uk

National Deaf Children's Society
15 Dufferin Street
London EC1Y 8UR
Tel: 020 7490 8656
Email: ndcs@ndcs.org.uk

OAASIS
Office for Advice, Assistance, Support and Information on Special Needs
Brock House
Grigg Lane
Brockenhust
Hampshire SO42 7RE
Tel: 09068 633201
Email: oaasis@hesleygroup.co.uk

Pre-school Learning Alliance
69 Kings Cross Road
London WC1X 9LL
Tel: 020 7833 0991
www.pre-school.org.uk

Picture Exchange Communication System
Pyramid Educational Consultants UK Ltd
Pavilion House
6 Old Steine
Brighton BN1 1EJ
Email: pyramid@pecs.org.uk
www.pecs.org.uk

Royal National Institute for the Blind
105 Judd Street
London WC1H 9NE
Tel: 0845 766 9999
www.rnib.org.uk